A SHORT HISTORY OF GUERNSEY

by

Peter Johnston

Published by
The Guernsey Society
2014

This edition published by the Guernsey Society
www.guernsey-society.org.uk

First Edition, 1976. Second Edition, 1982. Third Edition, 1987. Fourth Edition, 1994.
Fifth Edition, 2000. Sixth Edition, 2014.

Cover Design and Typesetting by Andrew Fothergill
Printed in Guernsey

ISBN 978-0-9928860-0-4

FOREWORD

When Peter Johnston first published *A Short History of Guernsey* in 1976, his intention was to provide a general chronological account of the history of the island which would appeal, not only to local people, but to all who might wish to learn something of the island's origins and heritage. Having been educated in Guernsey, he worked, for some years in sub-Saharan Africa before returning to the island in 1972 and, while teaching at a local school, produced his *Short History*.

Now once again living overseas, Peter, an enthusiastic member of The Guernsey Society – and at one time its Honorary Secretary – very generously donated its copyright royalties to the Society in order that it might be brought up to date and reissued to commemorate the Society's 70th anniversary which was celebrated in 2013. Bearing in mind the aims of the Society; "to promote, maintain and stimulate interest in all matters concerning the Bailiwick of Guernsey", it is Peter's hope that his *Short History* will continue to provide an easily accessible source of information on our island's past – and bring this information right up to its present.

Every effort has been made to incorporate the many changes which have taken place in Guernsey since the book was first published but, essentially, *A Short History of Guernsey* remains the work of Peter Johnston. Sincere thanks are due, however, to those who have made this new edition possible. In particular to Michael Paul who has led the updating of the content, Tanya Walls of Guernsey Museums who updated the chapter on Early History, taking into account all the recent archaeological findings; Stephen Foote, who has taken the lead in many of the other publishing activities required to get this into print; Andrew Fothergill, who has designed the cover and book layout; and the many others who have given guidance and advice on specific content issues.

We are also grateful to Guernsey Museum, VisitGuernsey, Priaulx Library, the Royal Court and David Le Conte for permission to use images from their collections to illustrate the book, as well as Michael and Andrew who have contributed their own photographs of the island.

Without their help, this new edition would not have happened, and the Guernsey Society is most grateful to them all. I hope that this latest edition will provide both information and interest to all its readers, upholding Peter Johnston's original objectives.

Keith Le Page
Chairman, Guernsey Society
2014

DEDICATION

In a book written for Guernsey schoolchildren in 1873, author unknown, the following quotation makes a suitable introduction to this short narrative:

"Je vous dédie ce livre dans l'espoir qu'il sera le moyen de vous faire aimer votre pays natal, ses lois, sa langue et ses usages, en vous racontant quelque chose de son histoire."

(I dedicate this book to you in the hope that it will be the means through which you will come to love your place of birth, its laws, its language and its customs, whilst telling you something of its history.)

CONTENTS

Chapter 1: Introduction.. 7

Chapter 2: Early History 15

Chapter 3: Feudalism and the Middle Ages 27

Chapter 4: Separation from Normandy.. 35

Chapter 5: The Civil War Period.. 41

Chapter 6: Trade: Privateering and Smuggling............................ 47

Chapter 7: Island Defences: The Napoleonic Era......................... 53

Chapter 8: Nineteenth Century Guernsey 61

Chapter 9: The Twentieth Century and Beyond............................ 71

Appendix I: Further Reading.. 84

Appendix II: A Chronology of Guernsey History......................... 86

LIST OF ILLUSTRATIONS

7 Map by John Seller 1783

11 The Guernsey Flag

13 Ormer (*Haliotis Tuberculata*)

13 Varieties of Guernsey Lilies
(*Nerine Sarniensis*) displayed
in Candie Gardens

14 The Early Neolithic Period
in the Channel Islands

16 Entrance to La Varde passage
grave at L'Ancresse

18 Statue Menhir at the Castel Church

19 La Longue Rocque at Les Paysans,
St Pierre du Bois

20 La Plaiderie archaeological dig,
April 1986

20 Model of 'Asterix', the Gallo-Roman
craft discovered at the mouth of St
Peter Port harbour in 1984

23 Medieval settlement at Albecq

24 Church of St Michel du Valle

26 The 13th century, as depicted on one
of the ten panels of The Guernsey
Tapestry displayed in St James
Concert and Assembly Hall.

28 Rural Guernsey landscape

30 Seat of Fief la Cour

32 Jurats of the Royal Court

32 La Table des Pions, Pleinmont

34 Le Château des Marais

34 Vale Castle

36 Barrière de la Ville, Smith Street

39 Illustration from Foxe's
Book of Martyrs

40 Charter of Queen Elizabeth I of 1559
reproduced by kind permission of
the Royal Court. © The Royal Court
of Guernsey

42 Castle Cornet with its donjon or
central tower, as depicted in a 17th
century painting

42 Castle Cornet as it is today

44 The Guernsey Falcon cannon

46 L'Invention, a Guernsey privateer

50 Old Guernsey house (c. 1400-1550)
with tourelle

51 The French Halles

52 Guernsey Militia uniforms

54 Coastal defence towers at L'Ancresse

54 Fort Grey, Rocquaine

56 Statue of Admiral James de Saumarez
at the National Maritime Museum

57 Portrait in pastel of Brigadier General
Sir Isaac Brock by Gerrit Schipper
(1775-1825) before his promotion to
Major General

58 The Vale Pond, the only remaining
undrained section of the Braye du
Valle

60 Former Town Hospital, St Peter Port

62 Part of the Commercial Arcade,
St Peter Port

64 The first commercial quarry,
Baubigny, St Sampsons.

66 World-famous Guernsey cows

68 Victoria Tower

69 Statue of Victor Hugo in Candie
Gardens

70 A steam tram meets a horse-drawn
omnibus by the Town Church

74 A Condor wavepiercer enters
St Peter Port harbour

76 The Reservoir, St Saviour's

78 German direction-finding
tower at L'Angle

83 Market Square, St Peter Port

96 Sausmarez Manor

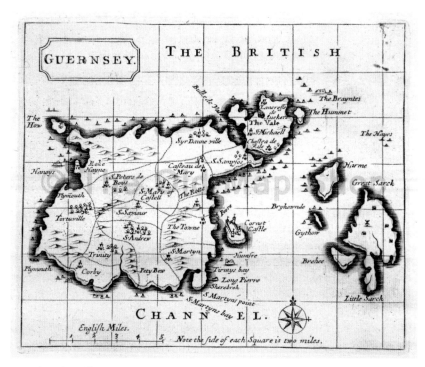

Map by John Seller 1783

Chapter 1

INTRODUCTION

Guernsey is one of a group of islands off the coast of Normandy which extend over an area of approximately 8,000 km² and are known as the Channel Islands. The group consists of two Bailiwicks, so called because the civic head of each group is called the Bailiff. One Bailiwick to the south of the group comprises Jersey (117 km² in area) with its offshore reefs and islets, the Dirouilles, Barnouics, Minquiers and Ecrehous. The other Bailiwick, to the north and west of Jersey, consists of Guernsey (65 km²), Alderney (8 km²), Sark (5 km²), Herm (1.3 km²) and Jethou, together with several smaller islands including Brecqhou, Lihou and Burhou. The last two named are not permanently inhabited, though Lihou is now leased by a charitable trust which is in the process of developing it for year-round use.

Guernsey is the second largest island in the group and is shaped like an isosceles right-angled triangle with the right angle in the south east and the hypotenuse facing west. The greatest length is about 15 km whilst the average width is 5 km. It has a population of approximately 63,000.

The land slopes gradually upwards from the north and west of the island which is flat and low lying, to a plateau in the south, some 100 metres high dissected by small steep-sided valleys. The south coast cliffs average some 75 metres in height and consist of very gravelly rotted granite gneiss which is extremely dangerous to attempt to climb.

The total area of inhabited islands of the Channel Islands is approximately 197 km² with a total population of around 162,000 which gives a density of approximately 820 per km².

The Channel Islands are largely self-governing. They have their own assemblies and therefore do not send representatives to Westminster. The group is the only remaining part of Normandy still owing allegiance to the English Crown, to which the islands' loyalty is directed, and not to the British Government.

For much of the period from 1066 to the present day they have remained possessions of the English Crown. They are dependencies of the Crown which are distinguished from the colonial and other overseas dependencies by their proximity to Britain and by the history of their relationship with the English Crown.

A decision made in 1801 by the British Government to separate government matters connected with the Channel Islands from government matters connected with the colonies may derive from recognition of these distinctive features. In that year Colonial matters were transferred from the Secretary of State for the Home Department to another Secretary of State. No change was made at that time regarding matters connected with the Channel Islands, but, in 2007, responsibility was transferred to the Ministry of Justice.

The Minister of State for Justice acts as an intermediary between the Channel Islands and the Crown: he advises the Queen on island matters, although both Guernsey and Jersey are responsible for their own domestic affairs. Defence and international representation, however, remain the responsibility of the British Government.

The island assembly is known as the States of Deliberation, usually shortened to the States. The name is derived from the French word *états* (estates), signifying the Crown, the Church and the People, from whom the assembly was originally summoned. It meets in the Royal Court chamber on the last Wednesday of each month, except August. Sittings usually last two days. There is a small public gallery where those interested may sit and watch the proceedings. An agenda, called the *Billet d'Etat*, usually in the form of a book, is sent to each States member in advance of the monthly meetings and contains all the States business for that meeting. The work of the States is coordinated by the Policy Council on which the Minister of each Department has a seat. It is led by the Chief Minister, who is, himself, elected by the States members at the first sitting of the States after an election. The day-to-day business is conducted by the ten Departments whose responsibilities are: Treasury and Resources, Education, Commerce and Employment, Health and Social Services, Culture and Leisure, Environment, Home, Housing, Public Services, and Social Security. Their Ministers are also elected by the States Members at a sitting of the Assembly.

The States of Deliberation is made up of 45 voting members called People's Deputies, two officers of the Crown who have no vote, and two representatives of the States of Alderney. The Bailiff is the President of the States and is appointed by the Crown. There is also a Deputy Bailiff who is able to exercise all the functions of the Bailiff should the latter be unable to discharge his duties for any reason. The Deputies are each elected directly by the island's voters for a term of four years. Previously, elections took place on a parochial basis, but the current electoral districts comprise: St Peter Port North, with seven deputies; St Peter Port South, six; St Sampson's, six; Vale, seven; Castel, seven; West (St Saviour's, St Pierre du Bois, Torteval, and Forest), six; South East (St Martin's, St Andrew's), six. Two elected members of the States of Alderney also attend and have full voting rights.

Alderney has its own States but Guernsey retains control over such matters as Health and Education. Sark, too, while also part of the Bailiwick of Guernsey, has its own government, known as Chief Pleas, whose members were elected democratically for the first time in 2009.

Guernsey's deputies may serve on several departmental boards and are responsible to the States for their administration. The Departments are served by a permanent civil service which has its headquarters at Sir Charles Frossard House in La Charroterie on the outskirts of St Peter Port.

The States have power to make *Ordonnances* (Ordinances) governing many aspects of island life; however more far-reaching measures, such as those creating new taxes or criminal offences have to be drafted as *Projets de Loi* (Bills), which, after approval by the States are submitted to the Queen-in-Council for ratification. They are not law in the island until they come into effect on a designated date and they have been registered by the Royal Court and lodged at the Greffe.

The UK parliament is said to be able to legislate for the Bailiwick without the consent of the States, but it is accepted that Westminster would only so do "in the circumstances of a grave breakdown or failure in the administration of justice or civil order". The UK can pass a law, the provision of which can be extended to the islands by an Order-in-Council should the islands wish to adopt the legislation. Finally, the Queen-in-Council can pass a law that will have effect in the Bailiwick. However, this Royal Prerogative has now fallen into disuse, with the consent of the States, having last been used in 1949.

The officers of the States who do not have a vote are HM Procureur and HM Comptroller, the equivalent of the English Attorney General and Solicitor General respectively. They are the legal advisers to the Crown and to the States and are Crown appointments. Other officers are HM Sheriff who is responsible for the maintenance of order in the States and HM Greffier who is Clerk to the States.

The States of Election is an electoral college composed of the members of the States of Deliberation with the addition of the 16 jurats, parish representatives and the island's rectors. This body is responsible for electing jurats of the Royal Court; therefore it only needs to meet whenever a vacancy occurs.

The Royal Court can sit as one of the following, a Court of Chief Pleas, a Full Court, an Ordinary Court and as a Court of Matrimonial Causes. The Bailiff sits as President, often assisted by a certain number of jurats depending on the type of case. There is no jury system in Guernsey as there is in England. The jurats exercise this function and to be elected a jurat is one of the highest honours that can be obtained in the island.

Besides the Royal Court, there is the Magistrate's Court, of which the Juvenile Court forms part. Magistrates have to be legally qualified.

Up to 1948, the Royal Court had a dual function, it acted both judicially and, when required, legislatively. It was from this that the States gradually evolved, only meeting when required for consultation. Eventually the States took over the legislative function of government whilst the Royal Court attended to the judicial side of affairs.

The Monarch's personal representative in the Bailiwick is the Lieutenant Governor who may attend States Meetings but addresses the Assembly only on leaving office. The office of Governor can be traced back to the reign of Edward IV who, in 1478, appointed a Captain of Guernsey directly under the Crown. More often than not Governors were not resident and the job became a sinecure, so a Lieutenant Governor was appointed by them to discharge the duties on their behalf. The last Governor of Guernsey was General Sir William Keppell (1827-1835), when the post was abolished after which only Lieutenant Governors were appointed, the first being General Sir James Douglas (1837-1842).

The Lieutenant Governor is appointed for a term of five years and it has been the custom for the Monarch to appoint high ranking officers from the Services. However, the method of selection was changed in 2011 and the post is now advertised and selection made by a panel in the Bailiwick which makes a recommendation to the Crown. The Lieutenant Governor is the official channel of communication between the Crown and the States, and represents the Crown at ceremonial functions, in addition to undertaking various statutory duties, issuing passports, fishing licenses, etc.

Parish administration can vary in detail according to the parish; therefore what follows is a general outline.

The administration of the ten Guernsey parishes is divided into two separate parts, the secular and the ecclesiastical. The secular part is run by the constables and douzeniers, with the office of Constable being the most important. The parishes each elect two constables; the one in office the longest is the Senior Constable who takes precedence over the Junior Constable. The constables are elected for terms of three years, but in practice, usually retire after two years as Junior and then Senior Constable. The exception is St Peter Port where they usually each complete the full term. Up to 1920 the constables acted as unpaid parish policemen receiving an official pocket-sized baton of office. Nowadays, since the establishment of a full time paid Police Force, the constables' duties are mainly of an executive nature; they include presiding over the meetings of the Douzaine, keeping the minutes of the meeting, dealing with all parish correspondence, settling parish accounts, receiving the parish tax known as the Owners' Rate and other parish taxes such as dog and shotgun licences. Towards spring each year a Parish Electors' and Ratepayers' Meeting is convened where the constables' audited accounts are presented to the ratepayers. Only those on the island electoral roll in the parish can vote at the meeting. All parish officers are elected by the electors of the parish, are sworn in by the Royal Court and are unpaid. The administrative and clerical work of the parish is now carried out by a paid clerk, thus relieving the constable of this work.

The parish council is known as the Douzaine and in eight parishes consists of 12 members served by the two constables. The Vale has four extra members to allow for representation of the detached part of the parish known as the Vingtaine de l'Epine. The St Peter Port Douzaine has 20 members including the two constables. The douzeniers and constables, each receive a copy of the Billet d'Etat, referred to above, which is discussed at a meeting held before the States Meeting.

Douzaine duties include inspection of the hedges along public roads after the twice annual hedge cutting in June and September, granting of *bornements* (alignments) for new walls, hedges and fences bordering roads, issuing of permits for building work to be carried out within 30 feet of the road, organising the collection of refuse, reporting on applications for liquor and bar lunch licences in their parish, care of parish roadside *abreuvoirs* (cattle drinking troughs) and the maintenance of parish property. The douzaine also prepares the budget to be submitted to the ratepayers at the annual parish meeting. If, as usual, the ratepayers vote the amounts requested, the constables apply to the Royal Court for a *Remède* (permission), to levy the owners' rate on all realty in the parish.

Douzeniers are elected for a term not exceeding four years, when they become eligible for re–election. The longest serving douzenier is usually the Dean of the Douzaine who presides over the ratepayers' and electors' meetings.

The flag of St George had been used as the official Guernsey Flag since 1907. Unfortunately it could not be used at sea since the St George's Cross is the flag reserved and legalised at sea for the use of an Admiral of the Fleet. Over the years the St George's Cross, when flown on land became confused with the flag of England, and it was felt that a new distinctive flag for Guernsey was needed. Accordingly in September 1983, the States appointed a Flag Investigation Committee "to examine the possibility of establishing a distinctive Guernsey flag". In 1985 the new flag was flown for the first time, the Cross of St George with a Norman Cross, in gold, superimposed. Together these are now known as the Guernsey Cross. For use at sea, a Red Ensign with the Guernsey Cross in the fly was introduced.

During the first half of the 20th Century, English was gradually accorded equal status with French as an official language and, in practice, is now used almost exclusively.

Guernsey Flag

French had been the language of the island for centuries until gradually in the 18th-19th centuries English replaced it. English had been spoken in the town since about the late Middle Ages with the arrival of English merchants and settlers who lived in the town area. It was seldom heard in the country areas until early in the 20th century.

Guernsey-French continued to be spoken in the country parishes and in St Peter Port on Saturdays, market day, until the late 1940s. This language, known also as Guernésiais, is closer to that spoken by the Normans than to modern French and, until relatively recently, was a verbal, rather than a written, language. Even in the early 20th century, children in the country parishes might only be introduced to English when they started school. A language not far removed from Guernésiais is still spoken in parts of Normandy and is understood by speakers of Guernésiais.

When Guernsey people did write, they wrote in as good a French as they could manage (the strongest argument for regarding Guernsey-French as a dialect rather than a language, according to Professor John Le Patourel). They had their Liturgie from the

16th century and their law books. The Greffe Records show the relatively high literacy of Guernseymen through the ages judging by the numbers who sign their names rather than simply making a mark.

Guernésiais, together with Jèrriais, is one of the Norman French versions of the *Langue d'Oïl* (Old French), which in turn descended from the Latin language. The purest and oldest version of Guernésiais is to be found in the south west of Guernsey, otherwise known as the High Parishes, as distinct from the Low Parishes in the north of the island, where the Guernésiais spoken is more anglicised and, in many cases, has more standard French forms and endings than that of the High Parishes. A brief revival of Guernésiais occurred during the German Occupation of Guernsey from 1940-45, but as most of the Guernésiais-speaking children were evacuated to England for the duration of the war, the link was broken and this, coupled with the influence of television, has hastened the decline to the extent that today it is only spoken by a steadily diminishing number of the older generation. However, efforts are being made to revive the language; it is being taught in voluntary classes in some schools and the annual Eisteddfod provides an opportunity for performances in Guernésiais, while some local media provide material for learners. In 2013, the States established the Guernsey Language Commission to encourage and support these and other initiatives.

Guernsey is, today, well known for the quality of its seafood and this is a facet of island life which extends back to our prehistoric ancestors. As will be seen in Chapter Two, the earliest inhabitants were hunter-gatherers and discoveries of quantities of sea shells, though mainly of limpets, in their middens show that seafood then formed a part of their diet. Sadly, the ormer, a gastropod mollusc belonging to the same family as the abalone, for which the island was once renowned is, these days, only rarely to be found as stocks have been diminishing for some years. Guernsey lies in the northern extremity of its habitat and now, by law, they may only be gathered at certain very low tides during the winter months. In addition to seafood, the very high quality of the milk and cream obtained from the Guernsey breed of cows is of special note, together with local horticultural produce. Local cuisine has in the main, tended to be simple and satisfying. Bean Jar, with its basis of haricot beans and pork on the bone, is both nutritious and nourishing. *Gâche*, which may be found in baker's shops, is a type of fruit loaf, and is particularly delicious when made with Guernsey butter, while *gâche mêlaïe* is a popular apple pudding.

Mention should also be made of the island's national flower, the Guernsey Lily, *nerine sarniensis*, a beautiful and complex bloom, and many theories have been put forward to explain why, for nearly 350 years, it should have been associated with the island, though actually originating in the coastal mountain areas of the Western Cape in South Africa. The mystery, however, remains unsolved.

Ormer (Haliotis Tuberculata)

Varieties of Guernsey Lilies (Nerine Sarniensis) displayed in Candie Gardens

The Early Neolithic Period in the Channel Islands

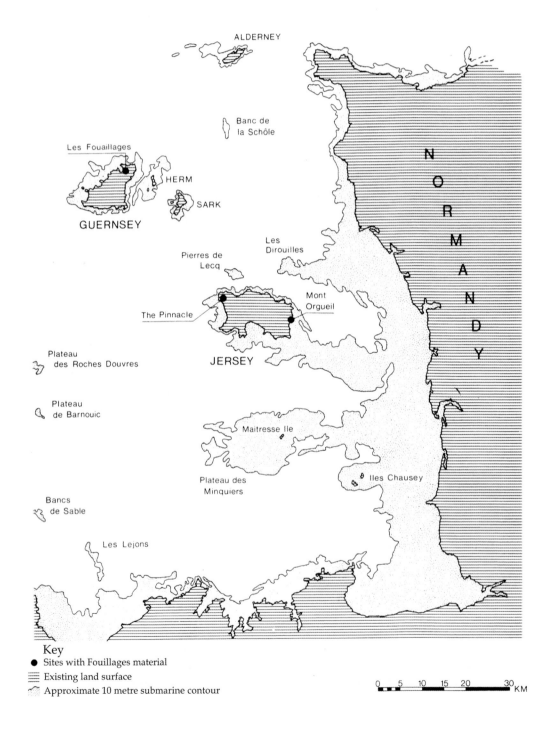

ALDERNEY

Banc de
la Schôle

Les Fouaillages

HERM

SARK

GUERNSEY

Les
Dirouilles

Pierres de
Lecq

Mont
Orgueil

The Pinnacle

Plateau
des Roches Douvres

JERSEY

Plateau
de Barnouic

Maitresse Ile

Plateau des
Minquiers

Iles Chausey

Bancs
de Sable

Les Lejons

N
O
R
M
A
N
D
Y

Key
- ● Sites with Fouillages material
- ≡ Existing land surface
- Approximate 10 metre submarine contour

0 5 10 15 20 30 KM

Chapter 2
EARLY HISTORY

During the past few years archaeological discoveries in the island have contributed greatly to our knowledge of Guernsey's prehistory and early history. The earliest evidence of human activity within the Bailiwick of Guernsey is to be found at Crévichon Beach on the island of Jethou. This site was identified in 2000 when a local man collected some distinctive flint blades, subsequently identified as Late Palaeolithic in date (c 10,000 BC). The flints are eroding from an ancient land surface accessible only at the lowest tides; when they were discarded the Channel Islands were still part of continental Europe.

Between 10,000 and 8,000 years ago rising sea levels cut the land bridge connecting Guernsey to France via Alderney. The high tide mark at that time was probably similar to the present low spring tide level; thus Guernsey's area would have been approximately 20 square kilometres larger than that of today, or as much as 60 square kilometres before the connection with Herm was broken. Virtually all this extra land would have been to the north, east and west and low lying, with a vegetation of mixed alder, elm, hazel and oak woodland and marshy land along the coast. Such low lying wooded areas provided good sites for early settlements, and Mesolithic flints have been revealed by erosion at various points along the coast. In 2001-2003 one such site was excavated on the north coast of Lihou Island. Over 5,000 flints and utilized stones were recovered and fragments of charred hazelnuts discovered in a hearth provided a radiocarbon date of c 7400 BC. People at this time were hunters and gatherers, probably leading a semi-nomadic life searching for small game and fishing along the coasts. This was about the time Lihou and Guernsey were separated from the Continent and many other such sites must have been lost to the sea.

One of the most remarkable archaeological discoveries of recent times was that of the Neolithic long mound, now known as Les Fouaillages, which was unearthed on L'Ancresse Common in 1977. The site was excavated in 1979-1981 and dated by pottery and radiocarbon samples to around 4500 BC. The pottery is *Linearbandkeramik* (Linear Band Ware), a type used by early farmers in the area of the Danube and this is the farthest west that it has yet been identified. Les Fouaillages is a highly complex monument because it was used over a long time period. The earliest features were an entrance façade of large slabs at the eastern end, a small sealed chamber, a larger open chamber and a cairn. These structures were contained within a triangular turf mound defined by a boulder kerb. Around 4000 BC the mound was covered with soil, stones

Entrance to La Varde passage grave at L'Ancresse

and turf, after which it appears to have been abandoned for some time. A large timber structure was constructed on the top in around 2500 BC. This was probably a temple or mortuary house and was used over a considerable period, falling out of use around 2000 BC. In the Bronze Age a settlement grew up close to the mound and the area was farmed. The field boundaries respected the - by now ancient - mound and continued to be cultivated into the Iron Age. By this time sea levels would have risen to roughly that of the present, inundating some of the old settled areas. In addition sand was being blown across what is now L'Ancresse Common, gradually covering what once had been a very fertile area. Some 1,200 years ago there is evidence of a massive sand storm which engulfed L'Ancresse, thereby preserving prehistoric monuments and evidence of past cultures under sand and eventually turf. It was in this way that Les Fouaillages came to be buried and forgotten.

There are other prehistoric monuments on L'Ancresse and elsewhere in the island which date from Neolithic times, some 5,000 years ago. The people who built these monuments were farmers. Farming allows people to settle and sustain larger communities. Agriculture originated in the Middle East and spread through the Mediterranean countries into central and northern Europe. It is these farming communities who were responsible for the building of tombs locally known as *dolmens* (dol, a table, men, a stone) and standing stones or *menhirs* (men, a stone, and hir, upright). During the Neolithic period dolmens and menhirs were erected in many parts of Guernsey. The dolmens comprise capstones, which can be huge, supported on large prop stones; there is usually an entrance passage and occasionally one or more side chambers. Most Guernsey dolmens have entrances facing roughly east. It is thought that they were orientated towards the sunrise during the time of their construction, typically around the time of the equinox and probably in the autumn after the hard work of the harvest was complete.

The remains of around ten dolmens survive in the island today, but from antiquarian records and evidence from place names it is thought that there were once many more. Unfortunately several were destroyed over the past 200 years, in most cases being broken up for building materials. The best remaining dolmen, although not the largest, is Le Déhus near Bordeaux in the Vale parish. It is a passage grave with a long tapering chamber, six metres long by four metres wide and two metres high. There are four side chambers. On the underside of the second capstone from the end is a carving of a man holding a bow; it has been suggested that this may predate the dolmen and was a carved menhir which had been incorporated into the tomb.

Another impressive tomb, La Varde, stands on a hill on L'Ancresse Common. It has a narrow entrance which opens into a large bottle-shaped chamber. Human remains were found in both tombs when they were excavated in the 19th century, the bone preserved by numerous limpet shells which had been deposited with them. The dead had been accompanied by grave goods such as pottery and stone tools and since the tombs had been used over a long period, these artefacts generally relate to the latter period of use around 2000 BC.

Other dolmens are to be found at La Platte Mare and La Mare ès Mauves on L'Ancresse Common in the north; Le Trépied at Le Catioroc near Perelle and Le Creux ès Faïes near Fort Saumarez, L'Erée, in the west. These prehistoric tombs were all excavated by the Guernsey antiquarian Frederick Corbin Lukis (1788-1871). It is to his early

Statue menhir at the Castel church

excavations and recordings that we owe a great deal of what we know about Neolithic Guernsey. He assembled a large collection of pottery, stone axes, querns and flint tools, some of which were unearthed from the tombs, but many were also found during ploughing or road improvements. On his death the collection was left to the States to form the nucleus of an island museum. Lukis was also responsible for preserving some of the dolmens still standing and his drawings of those he was unable to save from the quarryman's hammer are a very valuable record.

The dolmens and menhirs were regarded with great superstition by our ancestors and they feature in a number of local folk tales. The passage grave known as La Rocque qui Sonne was broken up for building stone by a Mr Hocart, however he was afflicted by a string of bad luck afterwards and both he and the stones ultimately ended up in a shipwreck which went down in the Channel. Le Creux ès Faïes – as its name suggests - was thought to be the entrance to Fairyland, while it is recorded that witches held their Black Sabbath at Le Trépied, conjuring up the Devil and dancing around the dolmen.

The finest standing stone or menhir is undoubtedly La Longue Rocque at Les Paysans. It is nearly four metres high and overlooks Rocquaine Bay. There are also standing stones on the

La Longue Rocque at Les Paysans, St Pierre du Bois

west coast headland of Le Crocq and in St Peter Port. As was the case with the dolmens, there were once others, but these were broken up for building stone, or removed because they were considered to be pagan idols.

Guernsey is fortunate in having two unusual carved stone pillars or statue menhirs. Today these female figures stand outside the churches of St Martin's and Castel, where they were erected in the 19th century, both having been found in the vicinity of the churches. Sites of pagan worship were often taken over by early Christian missionaries, who established churches on them in order that Christianity should replace, rather than compete with the pagan religion. Until recently little was known of the settlements of the monument builders and this has been the focus of some of the latest work.

On the L'Erée headland, near to Le Creux ès Faïes dolmen, evidence has been discovered of a settlement dating back to the Early Neolithic (c 5000 BC). This site was first excavated in 1998 and is the subject of an ongoing project which began in 2008. Large quantities of pottery have been recovered, but also stake holes and several hearths. Two phases of settlement have been identified: one of the Early Neolithic,

La Plaiderie archaeological dig, April 1986

Model of 'Asterix', the Gallo-Roman craft discovered at the mouth of St Peter Port Harbour in 1984

which was followed by a period of abandonment, and then a second of the Early Bronze Age (c 2000 BC). The later phase coincides with the final period of use of Le Creux ès Faïes tomb and it is likely that the tomb builders themselves were the occupants of the first phase.

In 1999 when the Royal Hotel was demolished on the seafront of St Peter Port, another Neolithic site was found. Excavations prior to redevelopment of the site revealed pottery dating from c 4800 BC in association with postholes and pits. Bronze Age occupation sites (c 2000 BC) have been excavated at La Hougue Câtelain at L'Ancresse, Fort Grey on the west coast and Route de Carteret in the Castel.

Work west of the airport, on the southern plateau of the island, has revealed more Bronze Age activity, including part of a trackway defined by the ruts from a wheeled vehicle, postholes, ditches and a hearth.

Across the south eastern headland of Jerbourg is a massive defensive earthwork. Jerbourg Castle consists of a series of ramparts and ditches across the narrow neck of the peninsula and dates from around 2000 BC. Part of the earthwork was excavated in 1978-81 and it was found to have originated as a small stone-faced defensive work which could be as early as Late Neolithic, however it was massively rebuilt during the Bronze Age. This complex site also possesses three medieval phases. Surprisingly it appears to have been out of use during the Iron Age, a time typically associated with the building and occupation of hillforts and promontory forts.

In recent years Iron Age sites have been discovered which have added greatly to our knowledge of Guernsey 2,000 years ago. In the dry summer of 1976, aerial photography revealed a series of crop marks at a field known as Les Tranquesous. Excavation proved these to be the remains of a late Iron Age settlement. There were a series of circular hut sites, associated with a double-ditched trackway, boundary ditches, gullies, pits and postholes. Pottery recovered from the site showed a range of locally produced coarse ware which was used concurrently with finer imported Roman wares. The site was in use from about 50 BC to around 200 AD.

Shortly afterwards, in the early 1980s, a complex of Iron Age ditches, pits and metalworking areas were excavated in the King's Road area of St Peter Port. The broken shards of a complete Samian bowl dating from the second century AD were found with the maker's name, HONORATI, on the interior. This would have been imported from the continent.

Further excavations in 2005-6 revealed some of the postholes of a round house and another trackway. This settlement has been dated to the Late Iron Age. Adjacent to it, although not contemporary with it, is a cemetery which has been dated by grave goods to c 300 BC. The soil being acid there was no trace of the skeletons and any organic materials did not survive, but the graves were sometimes surrounded by stones and several contained grave goods. 23 graves have been excavated to date and the grave goods include iron swords and shield bosses; bronze neck rings and, most recently, three beads which are probably jet. It would be very interesting to know how far this cemetery extends.

Until the latter part of the twentieth century evidence of a Roman presence in Guernsey had been lacking. The Samian dish from King's Road has already been mentioned and there are also *amphorae* (large storage vessels) of the first century AD from the above-mentioned Iron Age sites; this indicates seaborne trade with the Mediterranean during this period. Amphorae, from the region of Cadiz in Spain, have been discovered on the sea bed near St Peter Port Harbour and in 1984 the remains of a wooden boat dating from Roman times was found just outside the harbour entrance. The hull was some 20 metres long and contained the remains of a cargo of pitch. It was a flat-bottomed Gallo-Roman style craft constructed of oak beams fastened with iron and is a unique discovery. The remains of the boat, nicknamed "Asterix", over 100 beams, were lifted from the sea bed along with a quantity of artefacts. The discovery of several coins has allowed the craft to be dated to c180 AD. It is thought that the boat was built in Brittany and would have made regular trading runs from the Iberian Peninsula to France calling in at Guernsey. It was on one of these visits that it caught fire, burnt down to the waterline and sank.

At around the same time as the boat's discovery, excavations at La Plaiderie in St Peter Port revealed evidence of Gallo-Roman settlement. The site lay only 100 metres from the present sea wall and excavations revealed near continuous occupation for a considerable duration and suggested that the town of St Peter Port may have its origins in the Roman period. Three buildings of warehouse design were excavated, along with typically Roman stone-lined drains and gullies, together with storage and rubbish pits. Among the finds were a small Roman rouletted beaker, the remains of a trefoil spouted jug, glass and part of a Roman bowl used for crushing fruit on which was inscribed: "DIV I.S." Beneath the Roman level evidence of a timber dwelling from the Bronze Age was found and beneath that, late Neolithic flints.

In 1996 redevelopment of the market in the heart of St Peter Port gave opportunity to find out more about the town's origins. Archaeological excavations continued for several years, during which time almost the whole floor area of the Bonded Store was excavated, which meant working in between the massive foundations of the Victorian market building. Few medieval archaeological deposits survived, but there was considerable Roman material including large quantities of pottery and tile, parts of two Venus figurines and two engraved intaglios which would have fitted into finger rings. An iron smelting furnace was excavated and there were foundations of Roman buildings. The site had been heavily disturbed by the building of the markets and some of the Roman material had certainly washed down with the stream, which still runs through this part of the town. However, the quantity of finds along with the structural remains, strengthen the case for St Peter Port having its origins at least 2,000 years ago.

La Plaiderie and the Bonded Store, together with Roman pottery found at North Beach and Cow Bay, and the Roman wreck itself, suggest there may have been a trading settlement in the area between the White Rock and Fountain Street. A lot of evidence must have been destroyed in building operations over the past 100 years or so, nevertheless it is likely that more exciting evidence will be uncovered in the future.

It is thought that Christianity spread to Guernsey during the third and fourth centuries AD, brought by waves of Britons passing through from the West Country to Brittany. Around 560 AD the Celtic Saint Samson came to the island and it is believed that he landed on that part of the east coast that still bears his name; a church being built on the site where he preached. At this time, before the Braye du Valle was drained, the church was right on the seashore and up to the 19th century the sea used to reach the wall round the church. The parish churches all have dedications dating back to the

11th century, but some, if not all, existed before this time. Both the Vale and Castel churches have Roman tile incorporated into their walls, indicating the presence of a Roman building nearby, if not on the same site.

There were priories on the west coast islet of Lihou and at the Vale Church by the 12th century. These were daughter houses of the Benedictine Abbey at Mont St Michel; the abbey held much land in Guernsey during the medieval period. Vale Priory, now demolished, stood very near the present rectory and there are still traces of the walls built into later buildings. The fine carved stonework of the chancel attests to the importance of this church. The priory at Lihou was also destroyed and today stands as a ruin; the island is connected to Guernsey only at low tide and is entirely cut off for several days each month. Excavations at Lihou Priory cleared the collapsed building material to reveal a small but highly decorated church and a range of domestic buildings. Like the Vale Church, Lihou was decorated with carved limestone imported from Caen, it also had yellow and green floor tiles and painted window glass. The domestic range was small, but there were two storeys to one of the buildings and an *évier* (trough) for washing. Pottery and animal bone found at the site indicates that the monks lived well, although it is thought that at most there was only ever a prior and two monks living there. They would certainly have cultivated the land to grow vegetables and they had a dovecote for pigeon eggs and meat and fish traps on the shore. A number of burials were found both beneath the floor of the church and in an adjacent cemetery; interestingly the burials were not all of men, there were also women and children. So the church probably had its wealthy patrons.

As to medieval settlement, on the west coast at Grandes Rocques headland excavations in 1986 revealed two small oval buildings constructed from large beach pebbles. These remains are similar to buildings on St Helens in the Scillies and in Brittany and may

Medieval settlement at Albecq

Church of St Michel du Valle

have been used by monks. Pottery found at the site suggests a date in the early 12th century. A geophysical survey indicated that the settlement probably extends further to the south and west. Also near to the west coast, at Cobo, an early long house was discovered during building works. The site was occupied for a considerable time because four superimposed buildings were identified and dated by the pottery to between 800 and 1150. There was a circular hearth and an oven which may have been used in salt making. A bone gaming piece of Viking design was found, a unique find for the Channel Islands.

A further medieval settlement site has been excavated at Albecq, another west coast headland. Three stone buildings were found set around a courtyard, it is thought that one was a dwelling and the other two were of agricultural or industrial use. The foundations of two buildings can clearly be seen at the site today. The discovery of a small hoard of coins indicates that the settlement was in existence c1375. Traces of further buildings, enclosures and field systems extend out onto the headland.

The origin of the name Guernsey has been a subject of great debate with many different theories and explanations being offered. During the Dark Ages, roughly 400 AD - 1000 AD, Guernsey may have been known as Warnarsoy. In the Middle Ages there are several spellings all recognizable as the root of Guernsey, ie Grenesey, Garnereia, Gerneroi, Gernere, Gernereye, Guernereye and Gerneseye. One theory is that the -ey ending of Guernsey, Alderney and Jersey comes from the Norse *oy* (island). Whilst the *-hou* ending of Lihou, Burhou and Brecqhou come from the Norse *holm* (Islet). Thus Warnar(s)oy may have been Warner's Island, a Norse pirate or chief who perhaps seized the island sometime during the ninth or tenth centuries.

It is popularly believed that *Sarnia* was the Roman name for Guernsey and this has resulted in its incorporation in a multitude of applications across the island – if not the world! Recent research has shown, however, that this usage originated in an error made by a 16th century historian, William Camden, and it has been deduced from the Antonine Itinerary, a gazetteer of the Roman empire associated with various emperors in the second and third centuries AD, that Guernsey's original Roman name was Lisia, while Sarnia, or more probably Sargia, referred to Sark.

The origin of the ten parishes into which the island is divided is obscure, as is their age. Each parish is based on a parish church and, except for St Andrew's each has a sea coast. The first reference to the parish churches is in a document of the 11th century, but the parish boundaries could well be older than this. They may have evolved from the area the first Christian missionaries could administer, with natural borders such as streams or some prominent topographical feature in most cases. There is no satisfactory explanation as to why a portion of St Pierre du Bois and Torteval came to be detached. This has not happened in Jersey and all their parishes have a sea coast.

Another theory of the origin of our parish boundaries is to do with early agriculture. It is that the parish land area originally represented an agricultural unit based on the open field system of cultivation of an arable area surrounded by areas of waste land held in common by the parish. When the fief system was introduced in the island in the 11th century, it was probably imposed on an already existing parish agricultural unit.

The 13th century, as depicted on one of the ten panels of The Guernsey Tapestry displayed in St James Concert and Assembly Hall

Chapter 3

FEUDALISM AND THE MIDDLE AGES

From about the seventh to the ninth centuries the islands were inhabited by Bretons as part of the general northwards and westwards movement of these people from Brittany. During this period roving bands of Norsemen were making raids on the Normandy peninsula and the Channel Islands. These raids increased both in number and severity from about the eighth century onwards, but by the beginning of the tenth century they had begun to settle in these areas, under their Norse chief, Rollo or Rollon. Towards the end of 911 AD, Charles the Simple, King of the West Franks, drew up a treaty with Rollo and, at St-Clair-sur-Epte, Charles created him Duke of Normandy and ceded the new Duke all the lands which he had already conquered in the diocese of Rouen, Lisieux, Evreux, Bayeux and Coutances. Later on, the Duke acquired the valley of the Orme and as far westward as the River Couesnon. This is still the boundary between Normandy and Brittany.

Rollo died in 929 AD and his son William Longsword, Duke of Normandy, annexed the Channel Islands in 933 AD, and until 1204 they formed part of the Duchy of Normandy. Inevitably the Norsemen were drawn into closer relations with the West Franks. They were Christianised, their language became more Frankish or French, and they took over Frankish law, evolving a code of laws of their own known as *Le Grand Coutumier* which became the basis of the Common Law of the Channel Islands. It was not immutable, however, and over the years *Le Grand Coutumier* has changed considerably and elements of UK, international, and European law have been incorporated. Nevertheless, much remains of customary Norman Law, especially in matters relating to the land. A practice peculiar to Guernsey is the requirement whereby, in order to give their consent to sale of land, the respective parties have to appear personally before the court.

By 933 AD, the Norsemen or Northmen had become known as Normans, developing a style of architecture of their own, known in France as *Le Style Roman*. Though many of our parish churches have Norman foundations, the only original Norman construction still existing in Guernsey is thought to be the Norman arch at the Vale Church which dates from the early 12th century, but the complex architectural development of these churches - with the exception of St Philippe of Torteval - bears witness to work carried out over several centuries by masons brought to Guernsey from different regions of France and also from the English West Country. Prehistoric statue menhirs at St Martin's and the Castel act as reminders that the sites were often used for pagan worship long before Christianity arrived in the island.

Rural Guernsey landscape

The Norsemen being seamen had given Norse names to various features around the island, ie *guet* (watch tower), *étacq* (stack), *mielle* (sand dune), *dicq* (embankment), *crocq* (point), *banque* (low cliff), *vraic* (sea weed), *valle* (low-lying land). This applies especially to coastal features. Inland names are more French in form and date from the settled period as shown by *hautgard* (rickyard), *cotte* (sty), *belle* (paved farmyard).

The methods used by the Norsemen for dividing up their newly-won land was interesting in that the basic unit of land holding was the *caruée* divided into 12 *bouvées* which were further subdivided into *vergées*, 20 making a bouvée. There were 40 perches to the vergée but in the medieval period there were four vergées to the acre. A perch contained 49 square feet (3.36 m^2). It is somewhat confusing because the Guernsey acre in those days contained 7,840 square yards (6,555 m^2) against 4,840 (4,047 m^2) in the English acre. The vergée is still used in Guernsey, there now being approximately two and a half to the English acre, or about six vergées to the hectare. The system was worked out on the amount of land a man with plough team of oxen could plough in a given time. The caruée was the usual unit of land grant made to a favourite or relative of the King or Duke. The holder of this in turn gave smaller units of land, such as a bouvée of 20 vergées, to someone else to work on his behalf. This bouvée could have been further subdivided.

All rents from these subdivisions were due to the holder of the caruée who in turn had to pay tax on the whole caruée to the King. The caruée is equal to roughly three hectares.

Once the Vikings had finally settled in Guernsey they brought with them their laws, language and the Seigneurial system which was the basis of feudalism. The feudal system was the result of mutual agreements between the King or Chief, the nobility and the common people, for their common benefit. By agreement, the stronger members of society pledged themselves to protect the weaker in return for services exacted and rendered. It was a scheme well suited to the hard times in which they lived.

By 1066 the system was well established in the Channel Islands and in that year William, Duke of Normandy, became King of England after defeating the English King Harold at Hastings. From 1066 till 1204, except for a brief interruption, England and the Duchy of Normandy were united under a common leader who was both the Duke of Normandy and the King of England. The King or Duke, under this system, was able to take land for himself from which he drew revenues. He made grants of land referred to earlier, known as fiefs, to his followers in return for service and manpower in time of war. Each fief was held by a Seigneur who lived in a manor. Everyone who lived on a fief was his tenants even if they owned their own property. The Seigneurs were either members of the Norman nobility or Bishops and Abbots of religious houses. In those days the church was second only to the King in land ownership. There were two types of fiefs, the *fief haubert* and the *fief subalterne*. With the former, homage was owed direct to the King and when required the Seigneur had to supply a fully armed horseman accompanied by two or three squires. The fief subalterne's Seigneurs had to supply one lightly armed vassal only. As his fief was a minor one he paid homage to an overlord instead of directly to the King.

The first recorded grant of the island to Norman overlords is dated 1028 AD when Duke Robert is said to have divided Guernsey into two large fiefs: each containing about 19,000 vergées, one held by Nigel de Saint-Sauveur, Vicomte du Cotentin, who held the parishes of St Peter Port, St Sampson's, St Martin's, the Forest, St Andrew's and Torteval. The second fief was held by Ranulf Fitz-Anchetil, Vicomte du Bessin who held the remaining parishes of the Vale, Castel, St Saviour's and St Pierre du Bois. It is significant that the boundaries of these two former fiefs coincide with the present parish boundaries. Some years later, for some unknown reason, the fief held by Fitz-Anchetil was granted to the Abbey of Mont St Michel which established the Vale Church known as St Michel du Valle.

The tenants of fiefs owed rent and service to their Seigneurs in return for protection. The rent was paid in kind in the form of capons, eggs, fowls and grain, to name but a few.

Henry III ordered an enquiry into the customs and feudal servitudes of Guernsey in 1248 which gives us an idea of the rents and services paid by tenants to the Seigneurs of Crown Fiefs. Each tenant paid *champart*. This was one sheaf in twelve of his harvest and it went to the Seigneur. The tenant had to use his own cart to send the champart to the King's *grange* (store) which was situated in La Plaiderie in town. Once this was done the tenant was entitled to a meal at the King's expense and to receive the sum of nine deniers, which in those days may have been the equivalent of a fair day's wage for an agricultural worker. This payment was paid out of *pannage* which was a due paid for the privilege of pasturing pigs in the fief woods. This amounted to a tax of one denier for every pig with forked bristles which had to be paid as soon as pannage had been declared and cried in the market. In this period the market was held at the Landes du Marché on the Camp du Roi (Crown Land) during the summer months of March to September. During the winter it was held outside the Castel church.

The more important fiefs had their own mill and the tenants were required to grind their corn there. The tenant was obliged to send a man to guard the grange, the granary and the threshing floor. In return for this service he received the straw from each twenty fifth sheaf and was entitled to dine at the King's expense on Royal Fiefs Sundays and double feast days.

According to the Extentes of Guernsey, 1248 and 1331, cereals were measured in accordance with the following scale:

five quints .... one denerel

three denerels .... one cabot or cabotel

two cabotels or six denerels........ one bushel

four bushels .... one quarter

There were two measures in use, great and small. Great measure was in accordance with the above scale whilst in small measure the bushel and the quarter contained five and a half and 22 denerels respectively. But measures seemed to vary slightly according to the Fief. For example, in Le Fief Le Comte there appeared to be five denerels to the bushel. However, the denerel seemed to be a fixed measure whilst the bushel and quarter varied with the number of denerels they contained.

Like all his Seigneurs the King had the rights of *fouage* (hearth tax), pannage, and *verp*, a duty on all animals straying on to Crown pastures. He also had a percentage on all transfers or successions of land on his fiefs. Where a Crown fief bordered the coast he had the right of *varech* (wrecks), and *esperquerie*, the privilege of first choice of all

Seat of Fief La Cour

congers and mackerel caught by his tenants. In those days fishing was the principal means of livelihood of the poorer people in the community who salted and dried the fish before exporting them to England and Normandy to be eaten during the large number of meatless days required by the Roman Catholic Church. While being dried the fish were split open and held apart by pieces of wood called perches. This was corrupted to *esperques*, *pêqueries*, and eventually, *pézeries*, place names found only in the Channel Islands.

Fief Le Roi (The King's Fief), once held by Nigel de Saint-Sauveur, and the Fief held by the Abbot of Mont Saint Michel, formerly held by Ranulf Fitz-Anchetil, were the basis of parish administration. Most of the Crown Fiefs were concentrated in the south eastern part of the island. Here the fiefs were subdivided into *bordages*. A bordage was primarily the tenement of a Bordier. Within his bordage the Bordier farmed the King's Farm and, amongst other financial duties, collected other rents due to the King. He also served summonses and levied distraits. Amercements were collected by the King's Prévôt who was elected by the community of the island. In short a bordage was the unit employed for the collection of the King's revenue.

In feudal days the Seigneur not only had certain well-defined obligations to his tenants but he was also duty-bound to provide the millstone and beams for the fief mill. With the passage of time these obligations have fallen away and fiefs have largely lost their raison d'être in these modern times. Many of the feudal obligations have been done away with and those that remain are being challenged as being irrelevant. Certainly, *congé* which was two percent of the purchase price of a house paid by the buyer to the Seigneur on all fiefs caused a lot of resentment. In 1979 the States voted to transfer all payment of congé to the Crown. The Seigneurs were to keep their titles and for five years received a tax free one percent as compensation.

Feudal Courts were known as *Cours de Chef Plaids* (Courts of Chief Pleas), and were held at a specially designated place on each fief. Some of the stone seats can still be seen and date back many centuries. There were at one time over 70 fiefs which held court, presided over by the Seigneur of each fief. Most of these have gradually been abolished but it should not be forgotten that it was from the legislative machinery of these feudal courts that the present system of government has evolved.

Today, the Royal Court sits as a Court of Chief Pleas with the Bailiff as president with a minimum of seven jurats, though its activities are very limited. A roll call of members and certain Crown tenants is held, though advocates and parish constables are obliged to attend only at the session after Michaelmas. The business of the court consists in the receiving of reports on matters such as the fencing of quarries, the renewal of licences of *Salles Publiques* (public rooms), *douits* (streams), aerodromes, and it has been agreed that the sessions after Christmas and Easter need only be held if necessary.

A record of all tenants and the areas of their holdings or perchages was made for each fief. This book was called the *Livre de Perchage*; a new one was drawn up at least once every generation by the douzaine for the Fiefs Le Roi, St Michel and others held by the Crown when requested by HM Procureur. This custom has now been discontinued. The oldest livre in existence is one for Blanchelande in St Martin's dated 1488, although it is a mutilated copy. There is a complete copy dated 1580 for that fief.

Jurats of the Royal Court

La Table des Pions, Pleinmont

A long established custom came to an end in 1837, partly through lack of finance, and that was *La Chevauchée de St Michel* which had its origins in Normandy around a thousand years ago. The custom spread to Guernsey with the Normans and the organisation of La Chevauchée eventually became the duty of the Court of St Michel du Valle. La Chevauchée was responsible for the keeping clear of the *Le Chemin du Roi* (King's highway) throughout the island and of certain of the sea defences. The whole of the Court took part, the sénéchal, vavasseurs, prévôts, bordiers, sergeants and all the Crown Officers including the procureur. They were all dressed in costume, mounted, carried swords and each rider was accompanied by one or two footmen called pions, according to rank. These pions could claim the privilege of kissing any woman they met en route, provided that the lady had not already just been kissed by one of the other pions. These pions were chosen for their good looks, but even so some received *une giroflée à cinq feuilles* (a slap in the face). The prévôts or sheriffs used a lance nearly four metres in length carried by a Porte Lance and any obstacle encountered such as stones of walls on each side of the road, overhanging branches of trees, meant a fine for the owner. This fine went towards the expenses of the dinner for all concerned at the end of the Chevauchée. One of the stopping places en route for refreshment was La Table des Pions at Les Pézeries, Pleinmont.

Livres tournois were the common currency on account in Guernsey and France in this period. Tournois originated from Tours in France and was counted in *Livres*, *sols* or *sous* and *deniers* (Lsd). Guernsey used French currency, francs and centimes, up to 1920 when the change over to British money was made, although for a long time before both ran concurrently.

Another Norman custom, abolished in Normandy in the 16th century, but still exercised in Guernsey is the *Clameur de Haro*. This is a means by which a person can stop an encroachment on his property or his rights from being infringed by the action of a third party. In the presence of two witnesses he must kneel and cry *"Haro! Haro! Haro! à l'aide mon prince! on me fait tort!"* (Haro! Haro! Haro! – come to my aid, my prince. I have been done wrong). Then he has to recite the Lord's Prayer in French. Once this has been done the subject of dispute is under the protection of the Sovereign until such time as the case can be brought to court. However, the protest must be registered at the Greffe, the island's record office, within 24 hours of the Clameur being raised. A court case must be made within a year and a day. A person can be fined for raising the Clameur without good reason. It is thought that the clameur dates from Duke Rollo's time and that originally the cry was "Ha Rollo!" which eventually corrupted to "Haro!"

Le Château des Marais

Vale Castle

Chapter 4

SEPARATION FROM NORMANDY

When Duke William of Normandy conquered England in 1066 and became King of England, England became linked with the Duchy of Normandy. The Channel Islands had already been a part of the Duchy for 133 years, though whether any Guernseymen took part in the Battle of Hastings is not known.

The recorded history of Guernsey really begins with the loss of Normandy by King John in 1204. John's withdrawal from Normandy left the Channel Islands in the front line and they had to then make a decision as to whether to continue allegiance to the French king, or to go over to the English Sovereign. That they chose the latter course was a combination of several factors. In Guernsey, as in Jersey, the Normans who had large land holdings in the islands and in Normandy or England had to choose which they felt were the more valuable. No doubt those who were resident and had large holdings in the islands decided to stay, especially if they also had large holdings in England. They would then be prepared to forfeit those they had in Normandy. Those who decided to return to Normandy forfeited their island properties, and any in England of course, to the English Crown. These were then regranted by John to some of his loyal followers who had suffered the same treatment in Normandy.

One man in particular had good reason for not wanting the islands to remain French. He was Pierre des Préaux. This was because in 1200 John had given him the Lordship of the Channel Islands, besides giving him fiefs both in Normandy and England. After the loss of the Duchy he forfeited his Norman estates through his taking an active part in the war against the French. This left him only his English estates which he would have lost had he done anything to displease John, such as going over to the French. So it could be said that it was purely self-interest on the part of the Seigneurs that the islands chose to transfer their allegiance to the English Crown. The ordinary people were not consulted. An important reason for John wishing to retain the islands' loyalty was their possible use as a base from which to embark on an invasion of Normandy at some time in the future. In order to retain this loyalty John granted the islands the rights and privileges that they had previously enjoyed, and continued to govern them in his capacity as Duke of Normandy.

Some time in the early 13th century Jurats made their appearance. As an institution they are related to the lawmen of some towns in the Scandinavianized parts of England and the *échevins* or *scabini* of some towns and rural communities in northern France, ie their function was to know and to declare the customary law at a time when oral tradition was considered to be quite as trustworthy as anything in writing, if not more so, since virtually only churchmen could read and write. And with all the changes since the 13th century, that is still their essential function. The earliest mention of Jurats is in a document from the Court of Windsor dated 1248 in which 12 Jurats were sworn to uphold the customs, rights and privileges of the island. However, the problem of the origin of the Jurats is one of the most baffling in all the medieval history of Guernsey.

An enquiry into the laws and customs of the islands was made in 1248 by Henry III, through the Warden, or Governor, of the Isles, who was appointed by the Crown and subject to its supreme authority. The return of the enquiry relating to Guernsey was in two parts. The first was a statement of the services, customs and liberties of the island, whilst the second was a statement of the laws said to have been agreed by John in 1213. These laws are known as The Constitutions of King John. In these constitutions the right to elect 12 sworn *Coronatores Juratos* (jurats perhaps) is mentioned; the office of Bailiff; and the fact that the islanders are not bound to do homage to the King until he came in person to the island, or within the Duchy of Normandy, unless he appointed someone to receive homage in his name, ie a Governor.

It would seem likely that the office of Jurat had existed long before 1248, or even 1204, but the main purpose of the report of the enquiry was to make provision for the administration of justice without a special writ, as it was becoming increasingly difficult for the King to send travelling Justices to Guernsey as had long been the practice. The Bailiff mentioned in the Constitution was probably the *Seigneur des Isles*

(Warden or Governor), in whom the judicial, as well as the civil and military jurisdiction over the Channel Islands was vested: It was not long before a separate Bailiff was appointed in both Guernsey and Jersey who exercised judicial duties as the nominee of the Warden. In order to give the necessary authority to documents and orders issued on behalf of the King by the Warden, a seal engraved with his Royal Arms was granted in 1279 by Edward I. Between 1290 and 1300 separate but similar seals were made for both Guernsey and Jersey.

In 1254 Henry III granted the Channel Islands to his eldest son who later became Edward I of England, on condition that they were never to be separated from the Crown; no one but Edward was to have any claim to them, and that they should remain in their entirety for ever to the Kings of England. This had the effect of annexing the Channel Islands to the Crown of England, although the French did not recognise this until some 200 years later.

Barrière de la Ville, Smith Street

In 1239 under a Treaty with France, Henry III surrendered his title of Duke of Normandy over the former Norman possessions. He only retained the title in so far as the Channel Islands were concerned and so it has remained until today.

With the separation of the islands from Normandy, life in Guernsey and the other islands between 1204 and the mid-15th century became very difficult. The French launched a series of raids on the islands bringing death and wholesale destruction. Apart from hit and run raids there were several invasions; crops were destroyed and the countryside laid waste. In those days this was disastrous for the inhabitants who had to survive through the winter on what they were able to grow and store from the summer harvest. A bad harvest was serious enough, whilst destruction of the grain store was a calamity. There are instances of feudal dues being reduced or even waived altogether because of these raids. Even the churches were desecrated and many inhabitants sought refuge in Castle Cornet, Vale Castle, Château des Marais, La Tour Beauregard and Jerbourg Castle.

What can now be seen of the Château des Marais, which is situated inland from Les Banques, dates probably from the second half of the eighteenth century and was built to counter the threat of attacks by the French in that period, but historical records suggest that the original structure on the site predated Castle Cornet which was built in around 1204.

The first recorded attack by the French was in 1214 when a pirate adventurer named Eustace the Monk led an unsuccessful attempt to capture the island. Towards the end of the 13th century the islanders petitioned Edward I for aid as a result of French raids which had resulted in the destruction of the town jetty, the sacking of the town itself and the killing of 1,500 people, including women and children. The churches were looted and, to add further injury, before they left, the French hamstrung all the horses they had commandeered.

The island was attacked in 1305, 1336 and 1338 but many raids were not recorded, such was their frequency. Living under constant raids must have become a way of life. Following a raid early in 1338, the French returned in the autumn of that year under Admiral Bahuchet and conquered the island, holding it until 1340 when they were driven out. They held Castle Cornet until 1346, when as a result of the capture of six English ships by a French Naval Commander, Maran Le Maronier who put to death all those on board, Edward III decided to recapture it. A large force of men under Geoffrey de Harcourt besieged the Castle for three days before they took it and killed the Commander and its garrison of 500 men.

The town, which by now had been destroyed for at least the third time, was ordered by Edward III in 1350 to be surrounded by a wall. There is no evidence or record that this order was ever carried out. However, the supposed sites of the gates remain, marked by stones called *Barrières de la Ville*, erected in 1700 by the Town Constables. This was done to mark the boundaries of the town for reasons to do with the right of inheritance. Also, around 1350, the Tour Beauregard was built on top of Tower Hill, whilst the north side of town was guarded by a tower called La Tour Gand near La Plaiderie. The exact site of this is uncertain. The town defences in general have remained a mystery until recently when traces of the 14th century defensive town ditch were revealed in a dig at Cliff Street.

Another invasion took place in 1356 when both the island and Castle were taken. A force of Jerseymen was collected by the Warden of the Isles and after a fierce battle, the Captain of the French force was captured. He ransomed himself for 80,000 florins and the French agreed to surrender the Castle in exchange for him, after which they were allowed to sail away.

A well-documented invasion took place in May 1372 as told in a ballad entitled *La Descente des Arougousais*. Charles V of France sent a force of 4,000 men under the command of Evan, or Owen, Prince of Wales, and Morelet de Montmaur. Evan had gone over to the French to avenge the beheading of his father by Edward III. The attacking force landed at Vazon Bay where the islanders were awaiting them, having been warned, so the story goes, by Jean Le Tocq, an early riser who had been tending his sheep. The first battle took place near La Carrière not far from La Houguette, in the Castel. The invaders proved too strong and the Guernseymen retreated towards town, making a stand on the plateau between Clifton and Vauvert, then wooded countryside. Here a bloody battle was fought somewhere near a lane now known as La Rue de la Bataille between Havilland and St John's Streets. Apparently there were so many dead on the battlefield that it was possible to walk over them and blood ran down the valleys into town. The islanders lost some 500 men out of 800 before retreating to Castle Cornet. The ballad does not mention French losses but they must have been considerable. Other skirmishes or rearguard actions were fought near Hauteville and Lower Candie but lanes supposedly marking the sites have since disappeared. They were Rouge Rue and Ruette Meurtrière; this last used to run through what is now Candie Cemetery. Evan besieged the Castle for three weeks before giving up, whereupon he sailed northwards along the coast to lay siege to Vale Castle where many of the people from that district had fled for protection. Briard, a monk at the priory of St Michel du Valle by the Vale Church, acting as an intermediary, managed to collect enough money, jewels and other goods to persuade Evan and his men to sail away with the booty.

From 1372 to roughly the end of the 15th century, a period of continued unrest between England and France, all the islands suffered from spasmodic attack by the French. This caused so much misery and loss to the people that Edward IV requested Pope Sixtus IV to grant the islands the Privilege of Neutrality. This he did in 1480 in the form of a Papal Bull posted on the doors of the cathedrals of Canterbury, London, Salisbury, Nantes, St Pol-de-Léon, and Tréguier, as well as the parish church of St Peter Port. (A notable exception was the cathedral of Coutances.) The islands then entered a long period of relative peace but little prosperity, although from the early twelfth century, the islands, and Guernsey in particular, had been involved in the wine trade between Gascony and England. Guernsey benefited most because of her sheltered anchorage at St Peter Port.

In 1689, William III of England refused to acknowledge the Papal Bull but, in fact, it had long been disregarded and the islanders no longer had any real need of the Bull's protection. By then, the Reformation had changed the island's religious practice from that of Catholicism to a form of Protestantism.

Before the discovery of the Newfoundland cod banks, the island's principal export had been dried and salted conger eels. This trade declined soon after the discovery of the cod banks, leaving the cottage industry of knitting woollen goods as the only substantial export. A large part of the island's population in the 15th and 16th centuries was supported by the bleaching of wool, spinning, and the knitting of stockings, caps, gloves and the sweaters still known as guernseys because of their distinctive pattern. The women carried on this cottage industry while the men worked in the *éperqueries*, the fish drying grounds. The Foulon district in St Peter Port was where some wool fulling was carried out, hence its name. The island's small sheep population could not supply all the wool required and, as the export of wool from England was restricted, the islanders were obliged to make do with what they had, and with what they were allowed under the rationing scheme based on population currently in force in England. Guernsey's population at that period could not have exceeded 6,000 people. Foreigners were not encouraged to settle, an Ordinance of the Royal Court stating that, "no one shall lodge any stranger to live in the island under a penalty of 60 sols, except as a servant". This was in the reign of Henry VIII (1509-1547) but was modified in the reign of Elizabeth I to allow fleeing French Huguenots to settle, because of their Protestant faith.

The Reformation in Guernsey caused much bitterness and religious persecution. Henry VIII expelled the monks and friars remaining in the island; Edward VI (1547-1553) abolished the Roman Catholic Mass and imposed a French translation of the prayer book on the churches. Naturally, when the Catholic Queen Mary I (1553-1558) came to the throne, the mass was revived and the new prayer book suspended, but by then the island was irrevocably committed to a form of Protestant worship known as Presbyterianism. In 1556, three women were burned at the stake for heresy. They were Catherine Cauchés and her two daughters Perotine Massy and Guillemine Guilbert. This was the infamous case where one of the women gave birth to a baby which was hurled back into the flames on the orders of the Bailiff, Helier Gosselin and Dean,

Execution of Catherine Cauchés and her daughters from Foxe's Book of Martyrs published in 1563.
(By courtesy of the Priaulx Library)

Jacques Amy, both anxious to demonstrate their strong adherence to their new faith. This was a period when many persons, mainly women, were burnt at the stake, possibly at the foot of Tower Hill in the Bordage, on charges of witchcraft and sorcery. When the Protestants returned to power under Queen Elizabeth (1558-1603) they were not as cruel but just as intolerant as their predecessors. In 1573, a man was flogged through the streets of the town for attending mass, and by the end of the century, all Catholics had been ordered to renounce their faith or to leave the island. The Presbyterian form of worship was strong all over the island and although Elizabeth strongly disapproved of the situation, she allowed it to flourish in order to retain the island's loyalty.

Until the Reformation, Guernsey had, for religious purposes, been under the See of Coutances in Normandy, the Bishop receiving all feudal dues from the church fiefs. This situation had existed since long before 1204, and Elizabeth I corrected the anomaly in 1568 by the transfer of the islands to the diocese of Winchester.

On 29th July 1559, Queen Elizabeth granted the Great Charter which combined the grants and confirmations set out in previous charters. It stated clearly the Privilege of Neutrality, and confirmed and approved existing laws and customs as practised in the island. This Charter put beyond doubt the freedom of the populace from all restrictions upon trade and traffic with Britain. It also safeguarded the measure of judicial and administrative autonomy the island had. This Great Charter is the cornerstone of all the privileges the island enjoys in relation to the United Kingdom today and it can be viewed in the Greffe, along with some of the earlier charters.

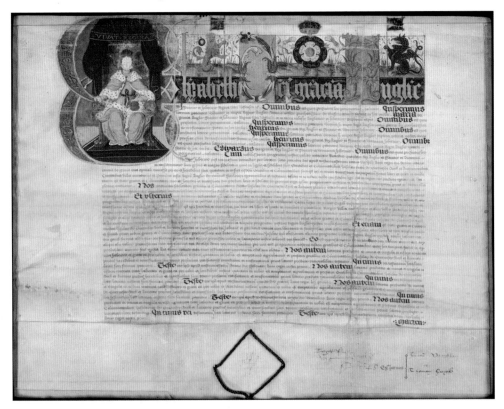

Charter of Queen Elizabeth I of 1559 reproduced by kind permission of the Royal Court. © *The Royal Court of Guernsey*

Chapter 5
THE CIVIL WAR PERIOD

Castle Cornet has often been the key to island history, right up to 1948 when it was finally demilitarised and handed over to the States by the British Government.

The Civil War was probably the most exciting period in its long history. The Castle's early history is very sketchy but it is known that in the 13th century a family called de Cornet occupied and owned an area of land south of the Town Church known then as *Le Bordage de Cornet*. It is assumed that the islet on which the castle was built also belonged to this family and was therefore eventually given their name. Cornet Street, formerly anglicised as Horn Street, also takes its name from the family bordage. Although there is no record of the date when the castle was begun, it is more than likely that the date was around 1204 after the island made the decision to remain with the English Crown. Before that there would have been little need of such a castle on that site. The first mention of the castle (no name) was on 29th October 1232 when John de Lambersard, the Constable or Captain of the Castle, was ordered to hand it over to Philip d'Albigny who had been appointed Warden of the Isles. Another reference is dated 8th June 1238 when it is referred to as *de Homet*. It was not called Castle Cornet until the reign of Edward III (1327-1377).

The medieval castle was considerably smaller than that which now exists, covering only the Barbican and Citadel areas and the ground between the Carey Tower and the Barbican. Between the Barbican and the Citadel was the Town Prison used up to 1811 when a gaol was opened, in the reign of George III, on part of the site now occupied by the Royal Court. This chapter will deal with Guernsey's part in the English Civil War, a war that divided the islanders for the first and only time between Crown and Parliament.

During this war the Royal Court of Guernsey took the side of Parliament, against the King and in doing so, nearly lost the island her ancient rights, privileges and constitution at the Restoration of the Monarchy in 1660. This was because the island had rebelled against the Sovereign to whom, as legitimate heir to the Dukes of Normandy, it owed allegiance (and its rights and privileges), and by submitting to a parliament to which it owed no allegiance at all, nor had ever done so. Article nine of Cromwell's Instrument of Government declared that both Guernsey and Jersey should send members to the English Parliament; this would have meant incorporation into the United Kingdom since Guernsey would have become part of Hampshire and, like the Isle of Wight, subject to English law. This was however not enforced when it was decided that the Channel Islands were not governed by English law.

Castle Cornet as it is today

Castle Cornet with its donjon or central tower, as depicted in a 17th century painting

What caused Guernsey to become so disillusioned with Charles I when, because of the island's link with the Crown, one would have expected the island as a whole to be strongly Royalist? The reasons were both religious and political and trouble between the States and the Sovereign had been brewing for some 75 years prior to 1643. Guernseymen who wished to be ordained into the church had to leave the island in order to obtain the classical education required. As French was their mother tongue, not English, they went to school in France where they learnt the Calvinist doctrines of the French Protestants which, on their return, they preached in their respective Parish churches. This was before the foundation of Elizabeth College in 1563 by Queen Elizabeth for this very purpose, as a Grammar School. As a result, to some extent, of this educational connection, numbers of persecuted French Huguenots fled to the islands, since many had friends or acquaintances there. As a result of their influence the Calvinist form of church worship, so reluctantly sanctioned by Elizabeth, became firmly established in Guernsey.

From 1570-1610 Sir Thomas Leighton was the Governor of Guernsey, a distinguished soldier and leading diplomat of his age. On assuming the Governorship, he immediately set to work on the Castle defences which he found very unsatisfactory. He also reported that the Militia was quite inadequate and that there were too many Normans and other foreigners in the island. The Castle fortifications were repaired, new guns mounted and the Militia reorganised. Unfortunately for most of the 40 years of his Governorship Leighton was at odds with the Bailiff, Jurats and the States over matters of financial detail, about which he was most particular. There being no income tax, his administration had to live on the Crown Revenues; any surplus going to the Governor. Leighton was very strict and careful in collecting the Queen's Revenues; nevertheless, on a number of occasions his view of what was legally due differed from that of the islanders. Because of this there were complaints concerning his taking too much of the Queen's Revenue for himself and of his misgovernment and tyranny. He was accused of imprisoning men without a Court Order and other violent acts; of making levies and exactions of money; of compelling people to obtain a licence before going on board a foreign ship and seizing foreign merchants' goods. Leighton had good reasons for his actions and answered all charges satisfactorily, whereupon they were dismissed.

During his administration the peaceful transition of Guernsey from Catholicism to Protestantism was achieved. Whether or not Leighton was a Puritan or a Presbyterian is not known. He certainly had a Puritan outlook on life but went to the Presbyterian Church. However in his day it was the only form of worship on the island. His greatest achievement was his part in the Calvinisation of Guernsey, since in those days the island's religious views came from France so there was no question of Guernsey becoming Church of England. Leighton has been described as a typical Elizabethan gentleman and of this there is not much doubt. He was a commanding figure and dominated both the political and religious life of Guernsey for over a generation. He was, however, very unpopular and perhaps his fault, if it can be called a fault, was the fact that he was probably too efficient an administrator for those times. The islanders resented his administration and it was remembered long after he left; his being a Crown appointment it was natural that some of his unpopularity rubbed off on to the Sovereign.

This bronze cannon, known as a Falcon and dated 1550, now forms part of a tableau in Castle Cornet. It bears the inscription "Thomas Owen made this pese for y'el of Garnsey". Despite this, it ended up in Massachusetts from which it was recovered only in 1985. (Photo: Jurat David Le Conte)

When Charles I came to the throne relations did not improve, mainly because of his offhand way of dealing with the States. Charles billeted 1,200 English soldiers on the islanders in 1627 and he could not pay the £4,650 bill run up over 19 months. This was a heavy loss for the poor islanders to bear. Disillusion with the King increased when the crews of two Guernsey fishing boats returning from the cod banks off Newfoundland were captured by Algerian pirates and held to ransom. Charles ignored the island's pleas for help and neither would he settle the earlier bill which could have been used to pay the ransom. The Royal Court and leading islanders might have remained loyal to the King if the Governor he appointed in 1621, Sir Peter Osborne, had been more sympathetic to the islanders' dispute with the King. He made no attempt to obtain their confidence, nor did he make much attempt to help them in their difficulties, preferring to stay in Castle Cornet, only leaving when he had official business in Guernsey.

By 1641, although the Bailiff and leading Jurats were still Royalist, they were wavering in their loyalty. Strong leadership by the Governor could have saved the day for the King as far as Guernsey was concerned and in all probability he would have had the island's support during the Civil War in England.

In 1643, Parliament issued orders for the arrest of the Governor and seizure of all forts and strongpoints in the name of Parliament. When this was not carried out, Parliament summarily deposed the Bailiff, dissolved the Royal Court and vested the Government of the Bailiwick in 12 Commissioners who all took turns to be Bailiff for a month. This action by Parliament was entirely unconstitutional because in theory it had no powers in the bailiwick. It would be difficult to say if all Guernseymen were against the King; certainly most of the leading families were since it was they who had suffered most under Leighton and Charles. Probably the average peasant was apathetic to the whole affair, only wishing for life to return to normal and to be left alone.

Sir Peter Osborne retired to the castle and although he left it in 1646, it was under siege for eight years and nine months. The defenders suffered many privations and were half starved most of the time. According to Pierre Le Roy, a schoolmaster of the time who kept a diary, some 30,000 cannon balls were fired into the town from the castle. This explains why there are no buildings prior to 1650 remaining in town. Many of those built just after the Civil War were swept away in the general reconstruction of the town 200 years later.

One of the most famous exploits of the war was the kidnapping of three of the Parliamentary Commissioners, Peter de Beauvoir des Granges, Peter Carey and James de Havilland. They were lured on board a supposedly parliamentary ship in Fermain Bay which promptly took them to the castle. After months of captivity they managed to escape from *La Tour Carrée* (the square tower) then situated at the southern tip of the castle, just half an hour before the order came from Jersey for their execution.

Jersey had remained Royalist and was able therefore to supply the castle by sea from time to time. This state of affairs continued until 15th December 1651 when Jersey surrendered to the Parliamentary forces. Castle Cornet, seeing that further resistance was useless, followed suit on December 19th. It was the last Royalist stronghold in the British Isles to surrender to Parliament.

With the Monarchy abolished, the fate of the Channel Islands was in the balance, Cromwell was styled *Son Altesse* (His Highness) in documents and all Fiefs du Roi became known, for the Commonwealth Period, as Fiefs de L'Etat.

On 31st May 1660 with the restoration of Charles II, things looked bleak for Guernsey. It had supported the wrong side thereby forfeiting all the rights and privileges granted to it under previous Royal Charters. Fortunately, several leading island families had remained loyal and some of them went to Charles with a petition from the islanders. This petition acknowledged the islanders' guilt and humbly begged a Royal pardon. This Charles granted, also restoring all Guernsey's rights and privileges as they had existed under his father. The island was extremely fortunate to get off so lightly under the circumstances. But no doubt Charles was only too pleased to get his throne back and wished to try to forgive and forget and not alienate those who had formerly opposed him. This was the closest Guernsey has ever come to losing her self-government.

The main event in the reign of Charles II was the explosion at Castle Cornet which occurred on 31st December 1672; lightning struck the *donjon* (central tower) on the Citadel in which was stored the gunpowder. The resulting explosion destroyed the tower and all surrounding buildings which included the Governor's residence, chapel, and banqueting hall, none of which was replaced. Several lives were lost, including Lady Hatton, the Governor's wife, his mother and daughter. Lord Christopher Hatton himself had a remarkable escape, being blown on to the battlements whilst still in his bed. From that date the Governors ceased to use the castle as their official residence.

The most illustrious political prisoner to be a guest at the castle after the Restoration was General John Lambert. Disgraced in 1661, he was exiled to the Castle for 10 years along with his two daughters, one of whom married Lord Hatton's second son.

When James II came to the throne in 1685 he attempted to reintroduce Catholicism to Guernsey by installing a Catholic governor and a largely Catholic garrison. He also insisted that mass be celebrated in island churches. The islanders resented this quite naturally and when William of Orange was proclaimed King of England in 1689 the island militia decided to act. Some of the island's important families formed a conspiracy with a non-Catholic officer of the garrison. When the day came for that officer's turn to be in command, the militia seized and disarmed such members of the garrison as were in St Peter Port.

At the same time, the Protestant officer paraded the soldiers who were in the castle, called the Protestants out of the ranks and ordered them to load their muskets. He then called on the remainder to lay down their arms, which they did and so the restoration of the Protestant monarchy in Guernsey was as bloodless as it was in England.

L'Invention, a Guernsey privateer

Chapter 6

TRADE: PRIVATEERING AND SMUGGLING

The island recovered surprisingly quickly from the upset of the Civil War, Commonwealth Period and the Restoration and the 200 years from the last quarter of the 17th century was a period of relative prosperity. During this period the town expanded, especially in the early 18th century, and many fine country houses and farms were constructed. Many of our fine Georgian buildings date from the latter half of this period and were built largely with the proceeds of the privateers.

In 1613 the island population was estimated to be in the region of 7,500; by 1727 it was 10,500, rising to 16,155 in 1800, the year of the first census. Of this last figure, 8,450 were living in St Peter Port parish. It took another 81 years for the population to double to 32,607 with again half living in the Town Parish, 16,538.

The age of Guernsey privateering began with the surrender of the privilege of neutrality in 1689. From that time until Waterloo in 1815, Guernsey seamen took to the seas as privateers. A privateer was defined as a vessel of war, owned and equipped by private persons to seize and plunder enemy shipping. The privateer had to hold a licence from the Government, called a Letter of Marque, which was issued to a subject who complained of injustice done to him by a foreigner. These letters allowed the commander of a merchant ship to seize enemy shipping either at sea or in harbour, and to take them and their contents as prizes, under the pretence of retaliation. This Letter of Marque was a very ornate, lengthy document on large sheets of parchment which carried the Sovereign's portrait and Royal Arms at the head. Attached to the letter was a wax impression of the Great Seal of the High Court of Admiralty. The terms of sailing as a privateer were very exact and the captain and crew were bound to a specific code of conduct, so that they were not pirates. There was a set rule on the distribution of prize money realised after each successful cruise. One fifth went to the King, two thirds of the remainder went to the owners, whilst the other third was divided between the captain, officers and crew. There were special awards of four guineas made to those men who first sighted the enemy ship or who were the first to board the enemy. The Letter of Marque was given to the captain of the ship and not to the owners who sponsored it.

Privateering was a perfectly legitimate and, for many, a very rewarding enterprise until it was abolished by international agreement in 1856. So profitable was it to Guernsey for some 150 years that it could be called an island industry because of the large numbers either directly or indirectly involved.

One of our most famous privateering captains was John Tupper who was eventually awarded a special medal in 1694 to reward him for his good services in destroying some French privateers. For the next hundred years Guernsey privateers did extremely well financially, especially during the Seven Years War, 1755-63, when the number of Guernsey privateers greatly increased and took full advantage of the war situation between England and France. In 1800 it was estimated that the island gained one million pounds through the capture of French and American shipping. In that year 35 more ships were fitted out in the island and added to the Guernsey fleet, carrying 250 guns and 1,716 men. These ships were sponsored principally by the families of Dobrée, Priaulx, Le Mesurier and Le Cocq. Their prizes amounted to a further one million pounds between them.

The assistance rendered to the Royal Navy in times of war by the Guernsey privateers was considerable. The Governor of Cherbourg wrote to Paris that both Guernsey and Jersey were the despair of the French at the outbreak of each war. So great was the help to the English that Westminster declared that the islands were almost entitled to be called one of the naval powers of the world, so large in number was the combined fleet of privateers. Many of the vessels were built and fitted out in Guernsey and a shipbuilding industry began, only to die out gradually towards the end of the 19th century. The main shipbuilding yards were at Havelet, St Julian's Rock, La Piette, Les Banques and St Sampson's. Guernsey indirectly owed to the privateers the introduction of what was for some fifty years from the late 18th century, one of the island's leading industries; that of smuggling or free trade as the islanders preferred to call it. Wine and brandy stored in vaults in town matured very well in Guernsey's mild climate, and together with her strategic position between France and England, combined to make Guernsey one of the chief entrepôts of smuggling. The British Government regarded smuggling as illicit trading and tried to set up a Custom House in St Peter Port in 1707. This was strongly resisted by the islanders, especially by William Le Marchant, then a jurat and later to become Bailiff. Another attempt at setting up a Custom House succeeded briefly around 1805, but the Lieutenant Governor had to issue a proclamation offering a reward of fifty guineas for information leading to the apprehension of "some evil-minded person, who had bored several holes in the bottom of one of the boats belonging to His Majesty's Revenue". So great was the trade of smuggling that a secondary industry became established; that of the manufacture of casks - small, easily carried kegs of 10 gallons. In 1805, there were 600 coopers engaged in making them and it was said that one family made £300,000 from the manufacture of such casks. The vaults and stores of town were overflowing and cargoes were actually hidden in fields above town under temporary coverings. Many of the town's Georgian houses, vaults and cellars of the quays and the Truchot are memorials to the Privateering and Free Trade era, at its height between 1770 and 1820. One of the most successful smugglers of the early 19th century was Jean Allaire, one time tenant of Jethou whose headquarters was at the Mount, a large mansion with vast underground vaults now the Lieutenant Governor's Official Residence in Queen's Road.

It was thanks to privateering and smuggling, together with their ancillary industries of shipbuilding and coopering that some island families made great fortunes, whilst many others were raised from poverty to considerable wealth. This change in fortune disorganised the old social order in Guernsey. These *nouveaux riches* naturally demanded the respect in life that in the past they had given to those better off than they. In 1777 some 20 members of the island's old aristocracy subscribed £2,500 and built Assembly Rooms above a market which contained stalls for butchers through open arches. In these rooms the subscribers and their friends held balls and parties, strictly for their own social order. These assemblies, as they came to be called, were governed by a stringent code of rules of behaviour and conduct. Membership was restricted to the old aristocracy of which about 60 families formed the island society who alone were entitled to enjoy the assemblies. They were known as the Sixties. The nouveaux riches, who by 1805 were at least as well educated, wanted to join, but their applications for election were turned down, and subsequently they became known as the Forties.

The social feud between the Sixties and the Forties lasted for roughly the first fifty years of the 19th century. Eventually the old Assembly Rooms were sold to Messrs Guille and Allès for the library with which they endowed the island in 1870.

An event occurred in 1787 which had a great effect on the religious side of island life and that was the visit of John Wesley, who was eventually responsible for the introduction of Methodism to Guernsey. The way had been prepared for this visit by Dr Adam Clarke who had spent three years, from 1786-88, at Mon Plaisir, St Jacques, the residence of Henri de Jersey. John Wesley spent nearly three weeks at Mon Plaisir preaching to huge congregations.

What of town and country life in Guernsey during the 18th century? Increased prosperity had made a considerable difference to the leading island families, many of them having both a town and a country house. In those days the town extended from Le Bouillon near the Longstore (which used to be a militia store) in the north, to the lower half of Hauteville in the south, from Fountain Street to Contrée Mansell, the Bordage and Mill Street. The present Market building was constructed in what was once the Town Rectory garden, and the Rectory itself was near Market Steps. Berthelot Street, narrow as it was and still is, was the main thoroughfare out of town to the Grange. Smith Street was much steeper and narrower than today; Fountain Street (*La Rue des Fontaines*) was only some three metres wide and the opposing houses were so close that people were able to shake hands across the street by leaning out of the projecting upper storey windows. The houses had been constructed after the Civil War and the majority was jetted in construction. Most of the town's streets were steep and very narrow, unlit, with no footpaths and at times little better than open sewers. There was a kennel or narrow ditch in the middle of the cobbled street to carry away the surface water and other refuse thrown down. Woodcock were shot in the fields above town where the Royal Court now stands, and there was only one church. The first church to be built after the parish church was that of Holy Trinity at Contrée Mansell, opened on July 5th, 1789.

Lord de Saumarez had a town house, the Square House, on the site of the sunken garden opposite the Old Government House Hotel. Between it and the Castel Church there were only eight houses. The main road in the 18th century was via the Rohais de Haut as Les Varendes did not exist. The Grange was narrower but it did have a footpath; Candie Road was just wide enough for a cart whilst *La Profonde Rue* (St James Street) was so steep and became so muddy after a storm that it was almost impassable. Only the lower town streets would have been cobbled. The sea came right up to the back of the houses of *La Grande Rue* (High Street) and Le Pollet, there being no Esplanade until the 1860s.

Old Guernsey house (c. 1400-1550) with tourelle

Most of the island houses were small, except for those of the merchants and gentlemen of the Town. The rooms were low and dark, sparsely furnished with poor quality furniture. It was not until the end of the century that Guille, who had a factory in Pedvin Street, and other Guernsey cabinet makers began to turn out mahogany furniture of Chippendale and Sheraton design which became highly prized as time went on. Furniture consisted of trestle tables, chairs and the green bed of dry fern raised about half metre off the ground. The parlour or living room of a house was of bare earth; even those of a gentleman had a sanded floor called a "Vale carpet". Because bare earth tends to sweat the floors were also covered with bracken which had to be changed every so often. The only means of light was the crasset, a primitive fish oil lamp which was boat shaped to catch the drips from an inner tray which contained oil from the liver of cod, conger eel or ray. There was a floating wick of singed or half burnt twisted rag.

In the countryside outside St Peter Port the island was divided into many hundreds of holdings, each the home of landowners whose houses were built of the material most readily available, the local granite, which varied greatly in colour in different parts of the island, and were very different in style from those within the town. Many of these attractive dwellings, which date approximately from the 15th to the 17th centuries, are still to be seen today and two of their characteristic features are the main entrance doorways with a rounded arch, which can also be found in Jersey, Normandy, and Brittany, and the *tourelle*, a semicircular turret enclosing a spiral stone staircase projecting beyond the rear wall. Clay mortar was used and the roofs were, originally, usually thatched. Interior features included massive granite fireplaces, and recesses in internal walls called *éviers*, a sort of medieval kitchen sink, and *bénitiers*, clearly a misnomer, probably used for hand washing.

Country people had very little to do with those in the Town except on Market days. They very seldom moved or ventured outside their own district or parish. This only served to accentuate parochial differences, especially in the Guernésiais language. It would be true to say for example that the vast majority of those who lived in the southern parishes had never seen or been beyond Cobo in their lives.

The country roads were appalling, very narrow, less than two metres wide and very tortuous. They were only wide enough for one cart to pass along and so when two carts met, one had to back up to the nearest recess called a *gensage*. Country journeys were made with pannier ponies, the women riding seated on large straw mats side-saddle, with stirrups slung across. The gig and four-in-hand were unknown until the following century. Those who lived in town seldom left it to visit the country because of the lack of transport and bad roads. A journey from Town to Pleinmont would have taken the best part of two days; but all this was to change for the better in the 19th century.

The French Halles

Guernsey Militia uniforms

Chapter 7

ISLAND DEFENCES:
THE NAPOLEONIC ERA

The Guernsey Militia probably originates from the necessity of having to provide some sort of defence against the early raids and invasions of the ninth and tenth centuries. There are no records to prove this of course but there may have been some sort of call-up system of the able-bodied menfolk who would have to provide their own weapons. Later on no doubt it grew slowly out of the feudal obligations of the tenants of a fief to give military service to their Seigneur and to the King. One of the privileges granted to Guernsey by King John was that Guernseymen were exempted from having to serve out of the island, except to restore the King to his throne or to rescue him from a foreign prison. At this period an order went out making the island contribute to its own defence; bishops, abbots, clerics, knights and vavassors to contribute a fifth of their annual income to maintain the knights and their men in time of war.

It was only during the latter part of the 18th century that the militia became really efficient and properly organised. Red uniform was worn for the first time in 1780 by all members, although they had to pay for it themselves. Fort George was begun in 1782 and finally completed in 1812 on land said to be the best in the island for the growing of corn. After the Seven Years War with France there was still the danger of a French invasion of the islands which were in a state of constant alert. Accordingly, 15 Coastal Defence Towers, incorrectly referred to as Martello Towers, were constructed to command those areas of the coast considered likely to be good sites for invasion. Many of these were built between 1778-79, long before the true Martello Towers, based on a circular fortress at Mortella Point in Corsica, were constructed in the 19th century in England and in British territories around the world. The Coastal Defence Towers were most numerous in the north of the island where the bays were thought to be ideal for the landing of invading forces owing to the gentle sloping nature of the beaches. They were built solidly enough to support six-pounder guns on the roof and to house up to 20 men. Three true Martello Towers were, however, built in 1804 on the west coast; Fort Grey (the "Cup and Saucer"), Fort Saumarez, and Fort Hommet.

With the Revolution in France on 14th July 1789, the threat of invasion became a real possibility which increased when Napoleon came to power some 10 years later. Because of this, for some 25 years from 1789 there was a frenzy of building activity so that by the Battle of Waterloo in 1815, besides the 15 Towers, there were 16 Forts and Barracks and 58 Coastal Batteries.

Coastal defence, or loopholed, towers at L'Ancresse

Fort Grey, a Martello tower protects the entrance to Rocquaine Bay.
Fort Saumarez can be seen in the distance

Many Coastal Defence Towers had powder magazines nearby. Many other preparations were made in case of invasion; cliff paths along the south coast were destroyed; alarm guns placed at the Hougue Fouque; signal stations erected and the militia were on constant alert. Both Guernsey and Jersey were so well prepared that no attempt at invasion by the French was made. One was planned in 1794, but this was called off at the last moment due to a combination of bad weather and the state of alert in the islands. A force of 20,000 men was assembled during the February of that year at St Malo with the express intention of capturing the islands and occupying them. Carnot and Robespierre were among the eight signatories on the decree.

The Duke of Richmond visited the island in 1785. He was Master General of the Ordnance and it was after him that the Fort and Barracks at Perelle were named. He was instrumental in producing the 1787 map of Guernsey by William Gardner, the first accurate survey of the island on a scale of 6 inches (15cm) to the mile.

In 1783, an Irish Regiment stationed at Fort George mutinied. This mutiny was quelled without bloodshed through a show of force by the Town Regiment of the Guernsey Militia. By this time, the militia had been reorganised into four infantry regiments; the East or Town Regiment, North, South and West Regiments. Formerly it had been organised on a parochial basis. There was also an Artillery Regiment. All men between the ages of 16-60 were liable to serve if called up. Training parades were obligatory.

In 1799, a division of Russian troops fighting for Britain was billeted in Guernsey as they were unable to land in England under the terms of the 1689 Bill of Rights. They were housed in barracks at Delancey, and during their short stay were not at all popular, getting drunk, rioting, stealing and in some cases entering cottages to drink the fish oil out of the crassets! They were so poorly provided for that they nearly died of starvation.

On June 8th 1794, the Signal Station at Noirmont in Jersey signalled the news that a naval action was in progress off the west coast. Captain James Saumarez, later to become Admiral Lord de Saumarez, was in command of a small English squadron of three frigates including HMS Crescent his own ship, and five small luggers and cutters. Just off the west coast of Guernsey he encountered five French frigates which heavily outgunned him. He therefore had no alternative but to make a run for the nearest friendly port. In order to save his ship he ordered the slowest to make for the south west of Guernsey whilst he and the other frigate HMS Druid, sailed to the north east of the island. The French were rapidly overhauling Saumarez and the Druid when he decided to steer the Crescent through a narrow maze of channels close to the west coast along Perelle, Vazon and Cobo. The French gave up the chase and their apparently certain prize because of the skill of the Guernsey pilot, Jean Breton, to whom Saumarez had offered a passage from England, having found him stranded in Plymouth. It was said that he was the only man in Guernsey to be able to steer such a course safely. Sir James did his best to secure a Government pension for Breton but the best he could obtain was £100 and a letter of appreciation. The Lieutenant Governor of Guernsey, Major General Small, presented Breton with a suitably inscribed silver gilt medal, and, later when a large memorial was erected to James Saumarez in Delancey Park in 1877, Breton's name was inscribed on one of the four giant plaques which were around the base. These plaques are now in Castle Cornet, the 33 metre high monument having been destroyed by the Germans in 1943.

Sir James Saumarez also fought in battles off St Vincent (1797), the Nile (1798), and at Cadiz. By 1801, he was a Baronet and a Rear Admiral; from 1803-07 he commanded the Channel Islands Naval Station based in Guernsey. He was promoted to Vice Admiral in 1807 and was Commander-in-Chief of the Baltic fleet (1808-12), during which time he gained the undying devotion of the Swedes. Then he became Vice Admiral of Britain in 1821 and Commander-in-Chief, Plymouth, from 1824-27. Finally, just before his death in 1836, he was created a Peer of the Realm in 1831 with the title of Baron de Saumarez of Saumarez in Guernsey. He was born in St Peter Port in 1757.

Statue of Admiral James de Saumarez, 1st Baron de Saumarez, at the National Maritime Museum

Other famous Guernseymen of this period were Isaac Brock and John Gaspard Le Marchant. Brock was born in 1769 in St Peter Port and lived, for a time, in the building which now houses Boots the Chemist. In 1785 he joined the army as an Ensign in the 8th Regiment and by 1802, was a Colonel in the 49th Regiment of Foot in Canada. In 1806, he was in command of British Forces at Quebec, and in 1811, was promoted to Major-General and appointed Administrator of Upper Canada. In 1812, on the declaration of war on Britain by the United States, Brock took decisive action, ordering the capture of Fort Mackinac on Lake Huron and, after a show of strength, accepting the surrender of the American forces in Detroit with 2,200 men and all its armaments and stores. A mere two months later, however, while leading his men in successfully repelling an American attack, Brock was killed at the Battle of Queenston Heights, near Niagara Falls. Often referred to as the Hero of Upper Canada, Brock's remains are interred in a vault in the base of a 56 metre column erected in his memory close to where he fell. He had been appointed a Knight Companion of the Order of the Bath for his success at Detroit though the news had not reached him before his death.

John Gaspard Le Marchant was born in St Peter Port in 1766 and he also entered the army as an Ensign, in the Royals in 1783. After service in Gibraltar and Flanders he eventually purchased a majority in the 16th Light Dragoons, a cavalry regiment.

Portrait in pastel of Brigadier General Sir Isaac Brock by Gerrit Schipper (1775-1825) before his promotion to Major General

He was interested in improving the efficiency of the cavalryman and to this end introduced a new lighter cavalry sword and a much improved sword drill, both of which were accepted throughout the cavalry service. For this he was appointed as Lieutenant Colonel of the 7th Light Dragoons. In 1802, after great effort he managed to establish a Royal Military College at High Wycombe, later moved to Sandhurst. He was one of the first to recognise that the British Army needed a trained officer corps and that the practice of buying commissions by the elite did not necessarily produce the best men for the job. He became the first Lieutenant Governor of the College and it was entirely due to his enthusiasm and efficiency that the college eventually proved its worth. He was there for nine years when in 1811, having attained the rank of Major General, he was given the command of a brigade of heavy cavalry in the Peninsular War then raging between England and France, He had already made many useful suggestions for the improvements of the British Army, one of the most important being the formation of the Staff Corps which proved very useful in the campaign against Napoleon. He gained great distinction at Llerena in 1812, but was tragically killed leading a cavalry charge at the Battle of Salamanca a few months later. He lived just long enough to see the complete success of the charge which resulted in 1,500 French prisoners being taken. He had killed six of the enemy with his own sword before a musket ball hit him in the groin.

During the early part of the 19th century the island owed many improvements to a new and energetic Governor. He was Sir John Doyle, a Major General and Lieutenant Governor from 1803 to 1816. The island received lasting benefit from his administration during which he tackled two great projects, in addition to reorganizing the militia and the island's defences. The two projects were the draining of the Braye du Valle and the improvement of island roads.

Up to 1806, the Clos du Valle was an island at high water, the sea flowing through a shallow channel from Grand Havre to the Bridge at St Sampson's. It was possible to cross the Braye by way of two causeways at low water, one of which was just below the Vale Church and was known as Pont St Michel; another one nearby was called Pont Allaire. It was just above the Pont St Michel that Doyle had an embankment built in 1807, the bridge at St Sampson's was filled in and the whole area of the Braye, together with its associated saltings or salterns was gradually drained. The Vale Pond is the last remnant of the former tidal channel.

The Vale Pond, the only remaining undrained section of the Braye du Valle

Along the edges of the Braye were salt pans from which salt was shipped across to St Sampson's and stored there. The owners had to be compensated for the loss of their livelihood.

The original beach line roughly followed the course of what is now the Route Militaire from Pont Allaire as far as another crossing place called Pont Colliche near La Bailloterie; and then along the Route du Braye where there was a fourth crossing-place at Rue du Tertre. The total area of land recovered was 632 vergées, six perches, or about 120 hectares. This was eventually sold for £5,000; Sir John Doyle presented this to the States on condition that it was used towards the improvement of island roads. This suggestion was not met with approval because the people begrudged the extra tax proposed for this purpose. The objections put forward were that the possibility of driving carriages on such roads would lead the islanders into extravagant habits; the destruction of property in order to widen and straighten existing roads (this was about the most valid reason); and it was argued that the bad state of the roads was a source of strength to the island because if the French did invade they would be hindered by them. This worked both ways of course and it was Sir John's intention to build roads that would enable his troops to be moved quickly to any part of the island in case of invasion so that they would be there to repel the French as they came ashore. This was his main reason for draining the Braye, in case the French used the Clos du Valle as a base from which to launch an attack on the rest of Guernsey. Once they had established a bridgehead there it would have been very difficult to dislodge them.

Sir John had his way with his road building programme and the first military road was built from Town through St Martin's, along the Forest Road, past Plaisance, through St Pierre du Bois and down to Rocquaine via L'Erée. The second road ran from Town via the Rohais and up Rohais de Haut, past the Castel Church and down to Vazon via Les Eturs and La Houguette. These two roads were only some 18 km long and cost an estimated £8,733 to build; £5,000 having already been contributed. Other roads were built once the States realised the value of good roads in opening up the country parishes. Doyle Road on the outskirts of Town was named after him. The islanders were so grateful to Sir John Doyle that soon after he left the island in 1816 a monument to his memory was erected on the Jerbourg headland. This was blown up by the Germans in 1944, and a much smaller, less impressive one erected in its place after the war. The original was about 30 metres high and had a platform at the top reached by steps up the centre of the tower.

Sir John was invited back to Guernsey in 1826 as the Guest of Honour at a banquet given for him by the States. By 1829 the States claimed to have spent some £30,000 on 85 km of first class roads and 28 km of second class roads.

The first official mail service between Guernsey and England began in 1794. The mail was carried in private ships via Weymouth and then by mail coach to its destination. Letters were charged according to the distance carried and the recipient had to pay on delivery. The letters had to be handed to a friendly sea captain for delivery to Weymouth and, naturally, he charged a fee for this service.

Former Town Hospital, St Peter Port

Chapter 8

NINETEENTH CENTURY GUERNSEY

The 19th century saw great changes in Guernsey. It would be true to say that the appearance of the island changed drastically over this period. At the beginning Guernsey was still a very rural community with the slow pace of life common to such communities. By the end the population had more than doubled from 16,000 to 40,000 thus destroying much of the old rural Guernsey, with ribbon development along the main roads and the spread of the Town far beyond its old boundaries. Two of the changes have already been mentioned, the draining of the Braye and the first military roads. Many more followed until by the end of the century Guernsey's road system was much as we see it today. Visitors began to arrive in ever increasing numbers, especially towards the end of the century, and several guide books extolling the island and its virtues, especially the mild winter climate, appeared in the 1830s and 1840s.

At the beginning of this period Daniel de Lisle Brock was Bailiff. He was the brother of Sir Isaac Brock and was Bailiff from 1821-42. His period of office saw some of the greatest changes for the better in the island. After the Napoleonic Wars ended in 1815 Guernsey, in common with England, suffered a post war slump. Guernsey was just beginning to move out of this period of depression when Brock became Bailiff. In 1831 the population of St Peter Port was 13,893 comprising 2,864 families in 1,728 inhabited houses. In the following year, cholera, which was rife on the continent, broke out in Guernsey in spite of precautions being taken. In the space of three weeks from October 16th to November 10th, 99 people died out of 365 cases. The death toll in Jersey was even greater with 341 deaths out of 787 cases of cholera.

Most of the Guernsey cases occurred in St Peter Port and were cared for in the Town Hospital which had originally been built for the poor of the town. The land was acquired in 1741 and it was in use by 1743, since then there have been many extensions. Because of its success some of the country parishes contributed towards the building of the Country Hospital in the Castel, not far from the parish church. Neither is now a hospital; the Town Hospital was a home for the aged until 1986 but has now become the headquarters of the Guernsey Police, whilst the Country Hospital was renamed Castel Hospital and became a specialist centre for patients with mental health problems. With the development of new purpose-built facilities in the island, the Castel Hospital is due to close by 2015.

Because of the cholera epidemic, improvements to the Town were speedily carried out, streets were widened and paved, drains were constructed and houses removed in

Part of the Commercial Arcade, St Peter Port

order to allow more light. As usual, apathy reigned supreme. St Peter Port Douzaine held their meetings in the Town Church and often passing parishioners had to be begged to come in so that there would be sufficient numbers present to enable a meeting to start. Nevertheless, the improvements were carried out with or without the consent of the majority of parishioners.

A new town was built at Clifton on land developed by Lord de Saumarez, one of the streets being named after him. During this period much of the old town changed from a residential area to a commercial one. Many of the town houses were converted into shops, especially those in Fountain Street, High Street and Smith Street. The Town Church was surrounded by old buildings, some only three to four metres away. Those to the north and west were removed and the street widened, thus creating what is now called Church Square.

With the progressive increase in population in the island, an extension of the shopping facilities in Town was required by the late 1820s and to this end an arcade was planned which necessitated the removal of most of the hill behind the lower part of La Grande Rue, or High Street, near the Town Church. There already was a small cluster of houses here which were demolished. A Jerseyman, George Le Boutillier, who had settled in Guernsey in 1804, was responsible for building the Arcade. 126,500 cart loads of material were excavated and dumped near Le Galet Heaume, now the South Esplanade, thus widening the area and enabling houses to be built on what was the old beach.

Unfortunately the venture proved too costly and Le Boutillier was ruined, and after some 50 houses were completed, several on the north side of the Arcade Steps were left unfinished and their outlines can still be seen today. Every house in the arcade has cellars and vaults many metres below ground level, whilst just below street level are a number of deep cisterns, constructed not only for domestic water supply but for use in case of fire.

Originally the plan was to have four entrances, the second entrance through what is now Beghins shop from High Street was never constructed. The arcades were to be covered with glass, hence their name, but the crash came before this could be done. This is why the houses were restricted in height and had to be flat topped.

Perhaps one of the most remarkable achievements of the early 19th century was the building of the markets where previously there had been houses and gardens. Prior to this, the fish and meat markets were held in the vicinity of the Town Church. In 1780 when the Assembly Rooms opened, the butchers moved to the market stalls provided beneath. In 1820 the States agreed to build a covered market at a cost of £5,500. £1,000 was already in hand but to cover the remainder it was suggested that £4,500 be raised by printing one pound notes, issued by the States. This was done and when Fountain Street was widened the houses on the north side were demolished to make way for the market. It was completed in October 1822 and opened by the Bailiff, Daniel de Lisle Brock, who had said, "Guernsey should make up only one great family whose interests are common. Only by union and concord can she enjoy firm and lasting prosperity"; a principle which still holds true today.

There were 36 shops in the market each paying a rent of five pounds. This meant that each year the States could burn £180 worth of their one pound notes and so with the

The first commercial quarry, Baubigny, St Sampsons. (Artist unknown)

help of a further £300 a year from the tax on wines coming into the island and paid into the "Market Fund", the States redeemed the original £4,500 in 10 years. This was an interest free loan which in the end produced an income of £180 a year to the States. However, in text books on Economics, this interest free loan is often referred to as "The Guernsey Swindle." Because in effect what the States did was a swift inflation affecting fixed income earners, ie the poor, followed by slow deflation, that of burning a set amount of notes each year for 10 years. In fact, it is little different from the techniques of Quantitative Easing used to stimulate the global economy following the 2008 Banking Crisis.

The stone trade which had started back in mid-18th century was now booming. St Sampson's Harbour was the centre for this trade, which, regrettably, destroyed many of our Neolithic monuments in the process. There were over 100 working granite quarries in the north of Guernsey at this time and during the 1830s an average of 43,000 tons of paving and other stone was exported per annum.

Shipbuilding was an expanding industry with, in 1834, eight boat builders and five ship builders in the island. Most of their yards were along the east coast from Le Galet Heaume to North Side, St Sampson's. This meant work for such ancillary trades as sailmakers, sawyers and ropemakers. In 1834 the principle of exporting corn to England duty free was upheld. This was very important to the island as much of the cultivated land was given over to the growing of corn. Cochrane's map of Guernsey dated 1832 shows 13 watermills and 15 windmills. Most of them ground corn; three were cement mills, there was a paper mill at Petit Bôt, a flock mill at Les Niaux in the Talbot Valley, tearing rags for the shoulder padding of coats, and one steam mill in the Charroterie for the grinding of wheat and the sawing of wood.

With the advent of steam, many more steam mills were erected over the following decades, as they were more reliable than wind and water mills. Gas lighting came to Guernsey on 5th January 1830 when permission was granted to Thomas Edge of London to erect a factory to produce hydrogen gas on his land at Les Amballes near the Bouet. Soon gas lighting was to be seen all over Town, both in shops and private houses and, for the first time, along Town streets.

Cross channel communications were improving, sail was gradually giving way to steam. The first steamer arrived in Guernsey and was called the Medina in 1823. Although she only made one trip she inaugurated a regular fast service between the island and Weymouth. Summer services ran almost daily with the journey to Southampton being completed in about 10 hours.

The improved service benefited the island from both the private and commercial point of view. With the Town given a new look, vastly improved roads and an increasing air of prosperity, the island was proving more attractive to the steadily increasing number of visitors, not the sun and sand variety as yet, but the well-to-do curious folk bent on improving their knowledge of the world or those naturalists whose hobby was botany, ornithology or just the study of nature in general.

Within a year of the Medina's first excursion, two paddle steamers, the Ariadne and the Lord Beresford were operating a regular summer service between the islands, Southampton and Portsmouth respectively. These ships were owned by a partnership of shareholders. In 1836 a company known as the British and Foreign Steam Navigation Company was running the services, giving way the following year to the Commercial Steam Packet Company of London.

The arrival of the railway from London to Southampton in 1840 greatly increased that port's importance to the Channel Islands. The Falmouth and Southampton Steam Packet Company commenced services to the islands in 1841. Eventually in 1843 the London & South Western Railway inaugurated their service from Southampton, having set up the South Western Steam Packet Company. Their first ship, the South Western sailed to the islands in August of that year. The Ariadne also operated a service between Torquay and the Channel Islands for three years until 1846. It wasn't until 1848 that the railways were allowed to actually run and own the shipping services. Their shipping advertisements didn't appear under the name L&SWR until 1851.

In 1846 the island had its first known Royal Visit when Queen Victoria and Prince Albert arrived off St Peter Port in the Royal Yacht. This visit was intended to undo some of the harm caused by a very unpopular Lieutenant Governor, Major General Sir William Napier, a distinguished soldier and historian of the Peninsular War. Soon after his appointment in 1842 it became apparent that not only was he irritable but he also displayed a certain amount of arrogance and a disturbing lack of tact and insulting behaviour that created serious differences between the people of Guernsey, including the States, and himself.

To commemorate the royal visit, a 33 metre high tower was erected on the site of the old L'Hyvreuse windmill west of town in 1848, and named the Victoria Tower. Previously it had been the site of a menhir which was broken up sometime in the 16th century when the windmill was constructed. Two roads were renamed in honour of the visit, La Petite Marche became Queen's Road and La Pierre Percée became Prince

Albert Road. Queen Victoria visited Guernsey again in 1859 and by that time Castle Carey was the residence of the Lieutenant Governors. In 1863 the statue to Prince Albert was erected at the landward end of the pier named after him.

Because of Guernsey's steadily increasing prosperity, the development of shipbuilding and the carrying trade, the old harbour was proving to be inadequate and after several schemes for a new harbour had been put forward in the 1840s, the States decided to adopt a plan by James Rendel, one of the most eminent engineers of the day. The foundation stone was laid by the Bailiff, Sir Peter Stafford Carey, on August 24th, 1853. Rendel died soon after but his plans were completed by a Mr Lyster and by 1870 the present harbour covering some 30 hectares had been completed. In 1862-3 the Bathing Places at Les Terres were constructed. The cliffs were cut back when the road was constructed and the rubble used as filling for the piers.

A tunnel, now an aquarium, was constructed at the end of Les Terres with the intention of continuing the road under Les Terres point and up to Fort George. This project was abandoned when the tunnel's roof threatened collapse. There was another tunnel about halfway along the road but this collapsed and there is now a cutting to mark its former position, near one of the Bathing pools.

The total cost of the harbour project was £360,000 and this included the construction of the North and South Esplanades where before there had been shingle beaches. These new wide thoroughfares for traffic to and from the harbour virtually completed the system of good roads begun by Sir John Doyle.

World-famous Guernsey cows

Under these new conditions the trade of the Town increased rapidly and by 1903 the cost of the harbour and associated works had been fully recovered. St Julians Avenue was opened in 1873, thus providing a Town bypass and the further improvement of communications between the interior and the Town.

The system was complete in 1935 when Le Val des Terres was opened. This road, built on land given up by the War Office, was largely financed by the Rev. P. T. Mignot as a means of giving employment during the depression.

In 1881 a lifeboat house was built on the Castle Emplacement. Previously the first lifeboat had been moored in St Sampson's Harbour, having arrived in the island in 1836. The Model Yacht Pond was constructed in 1887.

In 1855 the tower sea mark on Bréhon Rock was removed and a fort constructed midway between Herm and Guernsey. The British Government was worried about a French naval build up in Cherbourg at the time. In the same year, a 56,000 gallon reservoir under Havelet Road to supply the harbour with fresh water was constructed. A lavoir there had been removed in 1853 when the new South Esplanade was built. In 1859 the foundation of Les Hanois Lighthouse was laid.

In 1857 the islands set up their own service to Weymouth by forming the Weymouth & Channel Islands Steam Packet Company. They chartered two paddle steamers for this service, the Aquila and the Cygnus. This action spurred the L&SWR to enter into competition, although their service only lasted two years before they withdrew to concentrate on their Southampton service. At the winding up of the Weymouth & Channel Islands Steam Packet Company in 1889, the Weymouth service was taken over by the Great Western Railway who also took over the Aquila and Cygnus.

In 1889 the first modern mail boats arrived in the island. They were the GWR Antelope, Lynx and Gazelle. The following year it was the turn of the L&SWR mail boats, Stella, Frederica and Lydia.

The present harbour at St Sampson's was constructed between 1866 and 1880, much of the area on the North and South side being infill, most of the rubble coming from the nearby quarries. At one time St Sampson's Church was only a few metres from the beach.

One of Guernsey's most illustrious sea captains of this period was William Le Lacheur, who was born in the Forest. He was responsible for establishing the coffee trade, via Cape Horn, between London and Punta Arenas, the Pacific sea port of Costa Rica. The trip was made in 100-110 days by sailing clipper in the 1840-60 period. He died in 1863 and a fine ship named after him was launched at Sebire's Shipyard at Hougue à la Perre. William Le Lacheur is remembered in Costa Rica for helping to establish the Protestant faith in the Republic and some of his descendants still live in that country.

Another famous Guernseyman died in 1866. He was Thomas de la Rue, born in the Forest at Le Bourg in 1793. After serving his apprenticeship in the printing trade in St Peter Port he worked for several island firms before becoming dissatisfied with his prospects. In 1810, he decided to seek his fortune in London. The firm he eventually founded still bears his name and with the printing of high class playing cards it went from strength to strength, printing banknotes and postage stamps and establishing a world wide reputation for its fine artwork and printing.

Victoria Tower

Following Louis Napoleon's coup in France in 1851, Victor Hugo was one of the political refugees who sought refuge in Jersey. He was expelled from that island in 1855 over criticism of Queen Victoria's state visit to Paris, and arrived in Guernsey on 31st October accompanied by his son François Victor and his mistress Juliette Drouet. The rest of the family, including his wife, followed later. The following year he bought Hauteville House and it was here that he spent the next 14 years during which time he wrote *Les Misérables, Les Travailleurs de la Mer* (Toilers of the Sea), and *L'Homme qui Rit* (The Man Who Laughs). With the fall of the Empire in 1870, Hugo returned to France. Later on, a statue was erected in Candie Gardens to commemorate his 15 years of exile in the island.

Another noteworthy visitor from France was the great impressionist

Statue of Victor Hugo in Candie Gardens

painter, Auguste Renoir, who spent a month in the island in the autumn of 1883 and painted a number of canvases featuring, in the main, coastal scenes around Moulin Huet. But it would be remiss not to mention local artists whose work is internationally praised. These include Peter Le Lièvre (1812-1871), Paul Jacob Naftel (1817-1891) and William John Caparne (1856-1940) who worked in a former tramcar perched on a clifftop at Bon Port.

On 6th June 1879, a steam tramway was opened, running between Town and St Sampson's, the termini being at the Picquet House and the Bridge. Horse omnibuses however had been plying between the two towns since 1837 and eventually owing to the competition from motor buses which made their appearance in 1909; the line was closed down in June 1934. The buses were run by the Tram Company which had changed its name in 1888 to The Guernsey Railway Company. For many years there were several rival bus companies, Paragon, Bluebird, the Greys, Guernsey Motors and The Guernsey Railway Co. Over the years these gradually merged, until in 1974 The Guernsey Railway Company remained as the sole operator. However, in 2006, in an effort to reduce the use of private motor vehicles, the States became involved and purchased a fleet of new buses which are run, on their behalf, by a private operator.

The Guernsey breed of cattle has been sold and exported to dairy farmers in the United Kingdom since the late 18th Century, where they were prized for the quality of their golden creamy milk. The breed is believed to have evolved from the cross-breeding of Isigny cattle from Normandy and Froment du Léon cattle from Brittany, which were brought to the island by monks from Mont St Michel. In 1819, the States of Guernsey had taken steps to protect the breed, when it banned the importation of live cattle from France. By 1881, the Royal Guernsey Agricultural & Horticultural Society established a Herd Book for Guernsey Cattle to protect the purity of the breed, promote its improvement and enable purchasers of cattle to check their provenance. During the early years of the 20th Century, many Guernsey cattle were exported to the United States of America, and other dairy farmers around the world. Now there is a World Guernsey Cattle Federation linking members as far afield as USA, Canada, South America, Australia, New Zealand and South Africa.

On 31st December 1897, the Post Master General in England granted the newly formed Guernsey Telephone Council a licence to operate a telephone system in Guernsey outside the telephone monopoly which had been created in the British Isles. It was run as a department of the States until, in 2001 a decision was made to privatise the service and, a year later, despite considerable criticism, it was sold to an international company.

A steam tram meets a horse-drawn omnibus by the Town Church

Chapter 9

THE TWENTIETH CENTURY AND BEYOND

In 1900 a Projet de Loi, *L'Education Primaire Obligatoire* (Compulsory Primary Education), was passed under which all island children between five and thirteen years of age were obliged to attend school, three attendance officers being employed to keep a check on attendance figures. This Projet introduced compulsory education to Guernsey, although 50 years earlier an attempt was made to encourage children to be regular attenders. This took the form of an annual prize offered by the States for the best attendance.

In an attempt to centralise the island's administration, a new headquarters, Sir Charles Frossard House, was built in La Charroterie and opened in 1993, though other outposts of the civil service are still to be found in St Peter Port and elsewhere. The original States Office, an imposing granite building on the North Esplanade, dating from 1911, now houses an Information Bureau, together with a Bureau de Change, and other offices.

1914 produced a change to the east of the Town Church; three old houses, formerly inns facing the harbour, were demolished. They were the last of the old houses that once surrounded the church on every side but the south where the church yard was situated. This was removed and the venelle, a narrow alley, connecting Fountain Street with the harbour widened to become the seven metre wide road we see today. The lower end of Cornet Street was also renovated and in the 1930s the houses on the west side were demolished and the street widened.

On the outbreak of World War One in 1914, life went on very much as usual in Guernsey. There were some shortages of sugar and petrol but on the whole people were not very much affected by it all. The Guernsey Militia, which had been granted the title Royal by William IV in 1831, was disbanded in 1916 upon the introduction of conscription in England. The Act did not apply to the Channel Islands but the States decided to contribute to the war effort by making the men available for service overseas. The militia as constituted was not under the British Army's control in any way and was not liable for service unless the Sovereign was in danger. By disbanding the militia and reforming it as a new regiment of the British Army, the Royal Guernsey Light Infantry came into being. The First Service Battalion RGLI formed part of the 29th Division which was commanded by a Guernseyman, Major General Sir Beauvoir de Lisle. The Battalion suffered such losses at Passchendaele, Cambrai and Lys that they were withdrawn from the front and detailed for guard duties at GHQ until the end of the war. During the war a French seaplane base was established near the Model Yacht Pond. The RGLI was demobilised in 1919 and the militia reformed. The RGLI colours inscribed with battle honours now hang in the Town Church, and a war memorial to the dead was erected in 1926 at the top of Smith Street. In total, over 5,500 Guernseymen had served in the war and the number of casualties had a devastating impact on the island's families.

In 1923 the British Government invited the States of Guernsey and Jersey to make an Imperial War Contribution and accordingly a sum of £100,000 was voted by each island towards imperial war costs. The British Government apparently was not satisfied and asked for £275,000 a year from both islands. The States refused and offered a lump sum of £220,000. This was turned down and at the enquiry the States of Guernsey, through the Bailiff, brought to the notice of the Privy Councillors the privileges and immunities of the island. As a result of the statesmanship of the Guernsey Bailiff, Sir Havilland de Sausmarez, the British Government finally accepted the original offer of a once and for all payment of £220,000 in 1927.

In 1926 English was adopted as the official language of the courts and the States and the French franc was dropped as official coinage in favour of the English pound, the two currencies had been in use side by side for many years. In 1922 income tax was introduced at the rate of sixpence in the pound (2.5%).

Industry

After World War One there was a short period of post war slump, but it did not take too long before things were back to what would pass for normal. With the faster cross-channel passage brought about by the steamship, more perishable crops were able to be grown for export. During the last two decades of the 19th century, heated greenhouses were beginning to make their appearance, chiefly lean-to, for the cultivation of grapes, hence the reason why growing properties are still called vineries. The tomato, or love apple as it used to be called, began to oust the grapes soon after the end of the World War One. It had been introduced in the 1860s as a supplementary crop under the vines. This expansion in the tomato business produced a boom in greenhouse building during the first half of this century. Men were saving to buy a plot of land, erect some greenhouses and then, as money came in, to build their own bungalows. Many of the quarrymen in the north started in this small way. They worked in the quarries during the day and devoted their spare time to their smallholdings. Some quarrymen were part-time fishermen too. This expansion, coupled with a steady rise in population and little or no control over speculative building soon led to ribbon development along the main roads, thus irrevocably altering the face of the interior of the island for the worse. Such nucleated settlements that existed at St Martin's and King's Mills for example were soon swallowed up.

After World War Two, Guernsey's horticultural industry soon recovered and for many years was the mainstay of the island's economy. However, in the 1970s, it went into steep decline when the price of oil, essential for heating the glasshouses in order to produce their early tomatoes, rose rapidly so that Guernsey crops, with their additional shipping costs, could no longer compete in the UK market. Other crops, not requiring heating, were tried, ranging from flowers to peppers, from babacos to kiwi fruit, but only a fraction of this once all-important industry now remains. Guernsey's horticultural roots were, however, not abandoned, and while some growers continue to supply fresh produce for sale locally, others, adapting to the changing demands of the market, produce niche crops, such as clematis plants and fresh herbs, for export.

Other industries were developed which arose in part from the introduction of housing controls which encouraged wealthy individuals to live in the island and benefit from its lower tax environment. Among these were entrepreneurs who found a well-educated and willing workforce which enabled electronic, and other, manufacturers to establish businesses to set up here, exporting to the UK and other European countries. The major advance, though, was the development of a strictly regulated financial services industry which, taking advantage of Guernsey's low tax environment, quickly gained an enviable reputation and soon became the principal source of the island's gross domestic product. With its high value and low footprint, it is considered to be an ideal industry for an island where space is limited, and it is considered that diversity within the sector will reduce any apparent risk likely to be caused by an over reliance on one sector.

Flower growers developed a profitable business in the marketing of Flowers by Post which benefited from UK regulations enabling their produce, in packages below a certain value, to be delivered VAT-free to UK addresses. This successful local industry was, however, dealt a heavy blow when, as a result of major UK retailers setting up warehouses in the Channel Islands solely to re-export their manufactured goods in vast quantities, tax-free, back to the UK, the tax-free concession, termed Low Value Consignment Relief (LVCR), was suddenly removed altogether by the UK government. This had additional repercussions, not only decimating the fulfilment industry, as it was called, but also suddenly removing a large proportion of the bulk postal business on which Guernsey Post had come to depend.

As one might expect, since earliest times fishing has been a local industry and, with over 150 locally registered boats, the value of its catch in 2013, for example, exceeded £4 million.

Tourism

Guernsey's one-time second most important industry after horticulture had, together with the latter, been eclipsed by the rapid growth of finance and by changes in holiday patterns. The myriad little guest houses disappeared as holidaymakers demanded higher standards, and self-catering accommodation grew in popularity. Only hotels with substantial resources were able to upgrade their establishments sufficiently to meet people's expectations - including business travellers. The total hotel bed stock was reduced and, in consequence, the number of visitors to the island decreased, though the overall standards of accommodation were raised. The growth of cruising holidays from the UK brought about a rapid increase in the numbers of cruise ships calling at St Peter Port and annually some 90,000 people may come ashore, while Guernsey's marinas attract over 10,000 visiting yachts and cruisers each year. In keeping with the expectations of their clientèle, both local and visiting, the island's restaurateurs provide a wide choice of excellent establishments.

Transport

The years between World Wars One and Two had been a time of quiet prosperity; both the growing industry and the town were expanding rapidly, and the use of aircraft to provide additional transport links was rapidly developing. After the Armistice in 1918, sea planes were used to bring newspapers to the island on the same day they were printed. The first aeroplane to touch down was a blue de Havilland Moth which landed on the Fort Field (Fort George) in 1928. Also in 1928, a twice weekly service between Southampton and Guernsey was started by Calcutta flying boats. Later, an airfield was laid out at L'Erée with the help of a company founded by Sir Alan Cobham. This proved to be unsuitable and the States approved a scheme for the construction of an airport at La Villiaze covering some 312 vergées of good agricultural land. On May 5th 1939 it was officially opened.

By 1926, the limitations of the harbour facilities had become apparent and construction was started on the New Jetty at the White Rock, the work being completed in 1928 at a cost of £120,000. The use of the harbour has changed over the years. The Old Harbour and Albert Dock were, in the 1970s, turned into marinas, largely for visiting yachts, an increasingly important part of the tourist scene. Plans were passed in 1982 and a start made in 1984 on a three year project to turn the North Beach into a 30 acre enclosed marina. The scheme has provided nearly 1,000 parking spaces on land created to the north and south of the North Beach, the infill for which was obtained by dredging the present outer harbour of some 200,000 tonnes of material. The North Beach parking area has also provided much-needed additional space for container and roll-on/roll-

A Condor wavepiercer enters St Peter Port harbour

off traffic thus relieving the pressure on space at the White Rock. Ninety percent of the island's imports still arrive by sea and considerable effort went into reshaping the area of the Weighbridge to provide for the increased traffic flow from the harbour on to the island's roads.

With the reorganisation of the railway companies in Britain into four large groups in 1923, the L&SWR became part of the southern group known as the Southern Railway. The GWR was unaffected and continued to run the Weymouth service until the railways were nationalised in 1948, when British Railways was formed and took over the Channel Island shipping services. The boats used on the two routes included the St Helier, Isle of Guernsey, Isle of Jersey, Isle of Sark and St Julien, later to be joined by the St Patrick. These continued in service for another thirteen years.

Southampton was used as a passenger port for the Channel Islands for the last time in 1961, at the same time the new mail boats, Sarnia and Caesarea were brought into service by British Rail on the Weymouth run only. These were replaced by vessels offering a roll-on/roll-off service for motor vehicles in 1972. British Rail changed its name to Sealink in 1978 and operated services out of Weymouth and Portsmouth. It withdrew its services in 1986 and was replaced by a new company, British Channel Island Ferries which operated all its services, including freight, out of Poole.

In 1964 Condor Hydrofoils began a very successful passenger service between Guernsey, Jersey and St Malo with vessels travelling at speeds of 35 knots. Following the withdrawal of Sealink in 1986 they extended this service to Weymouth using larger, modern hydrofoils. In 1990 there was an addition of a 450 seat passenger carrying wavepiercer to their fleet operating at a similar speed to the hydrofoils. Early in 1993 a 574-seater high speed wavepiercer capable of carrying 84 cars was introduced on the Weymouth run, completing the 80 mile journey in two and a quarter hours. By the end of the 1993 season the last hydrofoil in service had completed its final run and was sold off. At the beginning of 1994 Condor took over the business of British Channel Island Ferries and when the route was put out to tender by the States in 1997, were successful in retaining the contract. Currently Condor, together with their parent company Commodore Shipping, operates regular high-speed services, employing roll-on/roll-off wavepiercers, between the Channel Islands, Poole, Weymouth and St Malo, in addition to a traditional roll-on/roll-off ferry which runs to Portsmouth.

Many changes have also taken place, over the years, in the field of air travel. Guernsey's main UK links with London, which had been served by British European Airways, were run by a succession of airlines, including BIA, Air UK, Guernsey Airlines and Flybe, the latter having originated as Jersey European Airlines. Aurigny Air Services, which had been established in 1968 principally running services between the main Channel Islands, grew to such an extent that when, in 2003, it seemed likely that Guernsey would lose its all-important landing slots at London Gatwick (Heathrow having already been dropped), the States stepped in and purchased the airline in order to consolidate the route, since when it has gained many plaudits with the travelling public. Meanwhile, in Alderney, Le Cocq's Airlink, which had been set up principally to fly goods in for the island's sole supermarket, was bought by the Guernsey-based Healthspan Leisure Group which was developing hotels in Guernsey and Alderney, and renamed Blue Islands. It currently operates services to Southampton and Jersey, with onward flights from that island to UK and continental destinations.

The Reservoir, St Saviour's

Water supplies

As early as the 1920s the States had considered measures for the avoidance of a possible water shortage after the very dry years of 1911 and 1921. The census figures for five decades from 1891 to 1931 were: 35,243, 40,446, 41,823, 38,223 and 40,588. The population was rising and what with the boom in tourism and horticulture it was obvious that a reservoir of some kind was needed. Early in 1939 work was begun at a site in St Saviour's where three valleys converged at Le Mont Saint. The intention was to construct a large dam and pumping station. There already existed a small pumping station and borehole on the site. Work ceased soon after it became inevitable that Guernsey was going to be occupied by the Germans and it was only restarted after the war ended in 1945. Eventually the 25 metre high and 300 metre long dam was completed early in 1947, and because of particularly heavy, and unusual, winter snows that year, was full by spring. The completed dam covered an area of 81 vergées and held 240 million gallons of water. Further potential increase in demand, led to the redevelopment of former granite quarries for water storage, and Guernsey Water, still a department of the States of Guernsey, now possesses a total of eighteen reservoirs, resulting in very satisfactory supplies of water for all uses. A beneficial side effect has been the development of an attractive Reservoir Walk around the original reservoir in St Saviour's.

Social Insurance

Until 1925 there was no form of state social insurance in the Bailiwick. There had been an unofficial Committee looking into the matter since 1912 and in 1925 the first social insurance law was introduced by the States. This law was called the *loi ayant rapport à la compensation pour accidents aux ouvriers* (law relating to the compensation for workers' accidents). This compulsory insurance provided compensation for accidents to workers earning two pounds or less weekly. It was followed by the Contributory Pensions Law of 1935 which extended benefits to Old Age and Widows' Pensions. Again it was compulsory for all those earning less than three pounds a week but gave those who eventually rose above the limit, the option of continuing to be insured voluntarily.

The Social Insurance Law of 1965 made insurance compulsory for all below the age of 65 and introduced unemployment and sickness and retirement pensions at 65. The retirement pension was replaced by an Old Age Pension in 1971. In 1979 the Social Insurance (Guernsey) Law 1978 came into operation and replaced the pensions flat rate contribution by contributions related to earnings up to an upper earnings limit. Other benefits now include family allowances, pharmaceutical and supplementary benefits including a contribution to general practitioners fees, full cover of specialist medical services, operations and hospital costs.

German Occupation

On the declaration of war in 1939 the States took precautionary measures which included the institution of food rationing, the issue of ration books, organisation of air raid and anti-gas precautions, and the militia was once again disbanded; this time, regretfully, permanently, as the move after the war to re–form it came to nothing. Everyone expected things to be very much as they had been in World War One and hoped that Guernsey would be able to sit things out without too much trouble. However this was not to be the case. The Germans swept through northern France and by mid-June 1940 were in Normandy. They occupied Guernsey on 30th June 1940 after a panic evacuation of some 17,000 people out of the 40,000 population. As things turned out it was just as well there were not so many civilian mouths to feed because food became so scarce towards the end of the occupation it was touch and go if many of those who had remained would survive. The situation in the island rapidly deteriorated towards the end of 1944 once the allies had retaken Normandy, thus effectively cutting off a whole division of German troops numbering some 35,000 men in the Channel Islands.

By Christmas 1944 food stocks, clothing, fuel and medical supplies were almost at an end when the Red Cross ship Vega arrived from Lisbon, Portugal, on December 27th with medical supplies and foodstuffs for the civilian population. The Vega paid further visits in February, March, April and May 1945 and if it had not been for this ship there is no doubt that many of the population would have succumbed from starvation and cold long before the liberation of the island. Finally, on May 9th, Vice Admiral Huffmeier, the German Commander-in-Chief surrendered. Soon after a small force of British troops landed and were received with great enthusiasm by the islanders.

A month after liberation King George VI and Queen Elizabeth paid a visit to Guernsey and it was not long after that the evacuees began to return home.

German direction finding tower at L'Angle

Government

Over the years the States of Guernsey have undergone considerable change. Immediately after World War Two, steps were taken to make the assembly more democratic and, following the passing of the Reform (Guernsey) Law 1948 the Jurats were removed from the States of Deliberation in which they had sat, by sole virtue of their office, for many hundreds of years. The objection was that as they sat both in the States and in Court they in effect made and administered the law. To take their place, and to provide continuity between elections, the position of Conseiller was instituted, but that, too, was abolished in 2000. Eventually, following the setting up of a panel to review the machinery of government, and after intense discussion over several States' meetings, a new structure came into being in May 2004. Although an executive style of government, as had been recommended by the panel, was rejected the new system is led by a Chief Minister and its make-up is detailed in the Chapter 1.

Health Services

In 1949 a new general hospital at Le Vauquiédor was opened by Princess Elizabeth and named after her. A States Enrolled Nurses Training School was opened in the grounds of the hospital in January 1967. Since then the hospital has been extensively modernised, with a programme of new buildings and alterations and extensions to the original premises. In partnership with the University of East Anglia it is now possible for locally qualified residents to participate in a full-time three-year course to obtain a degree in nursing. In Guernsey, many health related services, such as visits to a general practitioner, ambulance, accident & emergency, etc., are paid for directly by the patient, but specialist care, including hospital admissions and operations, are funded for residents by taxation. Visitors to the island are not covered and are advised to take out insurance.

Law & Order

The old Town Hospital, which had been built in 1743 as a Poor House, closed down in 1986, after serving as a retirement home for the elderly for some years. It was finally reopened in 1993, after extensive refurbishment, as the new Guernsey Police station. The old police station in St James Street dated back to the early 1950s and had become far too small for the expanding island force which, by 1994, numbered over 150 officers. The old prison too, built in 1811, had become too antiquated by modern day standards and a new modern prison at Les Nicolles in St Sampson's was opened in 1989 and allows for longer sentencing of prisoners who will be able to stay in the island instead of being sent to the UK, with all the extra costs to the Guernsey taxpayer which that entails.

In 2006, a new extension to the court house was opened on the site of the former prison to provide for the island's ever-increasing needs. Facilities in the Royal Court building had become totally inadequate and the new premises, coupled with the refurbished Royal Court, enable civil and criminal cases to be held in different buildings and for the States of Deliberation to meet in fitting surroundings.

Changing Times

In December 1958, Fort George, the site of Guernsey's principal defences in the 19th century, set on the high ground to the south of St Peter Port, was bought by the States from the War Office and later, against much opposition, sold to English developers who built a large number of very expensive houses on the site aimed at the open, or immigrant, market. This development formed part of a strategy to attract wealthy people to the island whose contribution to tax revenues would help to support the economy. In December 1959, the States decided to reduce income tax from 25% to 20%, at which level it has remained.

The death penalty for all crimes, other than treason, was abolished in the island in 1965.

Guernsey took over responsibility for the Post Office in October 1969 and the island began issuing its own stamps. It is not the first time that Guernsey has issued its own stamps; it had to do so during the Occupation when supplies of English ones, in use up to that time, ran out. The worldwide interest in stamp collecting made the establishment of a Philatelic Bureau a priority, since when issues of commemorative stamps have provided worthwhile revenue.

With the advent of decimal currency in 1971, Guernsey minted its own complete set of decimal coinage. Prior to this, copper coinage in the form of doubles, eight to a penny, had been in use since 1830. A silver 3d piece was minted from 1956, but although in theory Guernsey could have minted a full range of coins from early times, this was never done.

The Arts

There is no doubt that Guernsey's prosperity since the development of the finance industry has enabled the arts to flourish, and a turning point was, arguably, when the States were persuaded that the former church of St James should become a concert and assembly hall instead of a police station which is what had been proposed. The opening of St James in its new role in 1985 provided the island with a concert hall of the highest standards which has attracted many artists of international repute, in addition to providing a venue to which talented local musicians and other performers might aspire. The schools' music service has helped to bring on numbers of local youngsters who have not only contributed greatly to the quality of local performances, but gone on to become accomplished musicians in the wider world. Drama, too, has flourished in the island. The Guernsey Amateur Dramatic and Operatic Society, founded in 1927, continues to thrive while many music groups and choirs give highly professional performances. The Princess Royal Theatre of the Performing Arts which was opened in 2007 is run by the Education Department and enables youngsters to study full-time performing arts courses; while the graphic and creative arts also receive strong support from the International Artist in Residence Programme.

Guernsey's Museums provide comprehensive accounts of the island's history and include historic monuments such as Castle Cornet, while the period of occupation during World War Two is portrayed in detail by the privately owned German Occupation Museum.

European Union

In January 1972, following negotiations by the UK government, the position of the Channel Islands (and the Isle of Man) with regard to the European Union was embodied in Protocol No. 3 of the Treaty of Accession of the United Kingdom to the EEC. While Guernsey retains its own laws and system of taxation - for example, value added tax is not applicable - no customs duties are applied to goods exported to members of the customs union, but a common customs tariff is applied to goods imported from non-member countries. Thus, while Guernsey is within the EU with regard to the free movement of goods, it is outside for other purposes, in particular for non-customs-related fiscal matters. Additionally, though Channel Islanders are British citizens, they do not have the same right as UK citizens to work in continental EU countries unless they have specific links with the UK.

Increasingly, however, the Channel Islands have found themselves obliged to comply with rules and regulations set in Brussels to ensure that trade with members of the European Union can be maintained and in 2011 it was considered essential for a joint Guernsey and Jersey office to be established in Brussels to maintain closer contact with the community.

Financial Relationship with UK

In 1985 Guernsey, together with Jersey, accepted the principle of making a contribution to the UK Defence budget. Guernsey decided to pay for the upkeep of the Alderney Breakwater. The States also agreed to pay for overseas representation as required and to hand over all fees collected in respect of passports issued in the island. In recent years Guernsey has been paying for more of the services previously paid for by the British taxpayer. This has come about through the improving prosperity of the island compared with the prewar and immediate postwar period. For example the States Education Department now pays the going rate for all Guernsey students studying in the UK, and the Department of Health pays for UK services rendered to patients sent for specialist treatment. Guernsey's postwar prosperity has thus brought greater financial independence from the UK than in the past, with the island paying its own way in virtually everything.

Inter-island Co-operation

As indicated above, Guernsey is now starting to work more closely with its sister island of Jersey. As services become more complex and expensive the only way forward is for much more co-operation and liaison between the two Bailiwicks. It does not make sense from a financial point of view for the islands to duplicate certain services which could be shared. Independence need not be sacrificed as there is a lot to be gained by both islands by co-operation. This can also be extended to our near neighbour France in certain fields. Guernsey Electricity Ltd is the sole supplier of electricity to the island, which is either imported by subsea cable from the European grid or generated locally using generators at the Vale Power Station. The subsea cable link interconnection network originates on the Normandy coast from where it connects to Jersey. Power is then transferred across Jersey and on to Guernsey via another subsea cable. Guernsey Electricity additionally maintains a fleet of generators to ensure security of supply for the island and to meet any shortfall in capacity from the subsea interconnectors. The generators consist of five slow speed two-stroke diesel engines, one medium speed four-stroke diesel engine and three gas turbines, giving a combined installed capacity of 122MW. In the financial year from April 2011 to March 2012, for example, Guernsey's peak power demand was in the order of 85MW and the island consumed in the order of 380GWh of electricity, 82% being imported from the European grid with the balance being generated on island. A strategy of increased subsea cable capacity will enable Guernsey Electricity to continue providing secure and reliable supplies and with a reduced carbon level on the environment. Investigations are now also being made into the possibility of generating electricity through tidal power, taking advantage of the immense movement of the sea in local waters.

Environment

An issue which has long troubled local, and other, environmentalists is the disposal of sewage and other waste. After years of wrangling, an exhaustive scientific study has shown that waste water and sewage, which is discharged into the fast-moving currents of the Little Russel about a mile offshore, is dealt with by natural process which, ecologically, effectively takes care of it, thus meeting the most up-to-date EU standards. The disposal of household, and other, refuse, however, remains a problem. The system of landfill, burying this waste in the vast holes left in the north of the island by the quarrying of granite has inevitably come to an end with the last quarry being virtually full. After lengthy discussions and investigations, a decision was reached to maximise recycling and to ship what remains out of the island for incineration.

Population

One of the island's problems at present is that of overpopulation. With a density of around 970 per km² this is a problem and a number of remedies to try to stabilize the population are being considered. Solutions to the related problems of car parking in St Peter Port and the island's car population in general are also being considered.

Economy

Guernsey's chief sources of income are similar in many respects to those of Jersey. In order of importance these are as follows: International banking, tourism, horticulture and agriculture. The stabilisation of a low income tax, no surtax and many other benefits have all contributed to the popularity of the island and the problems this has brought with it. In 2002, the States agreed that Guernsey's 20% tax rate which, for so many years, had attracted business to the island, had become uncompetitive by comparison with lower tax regimes being introduced by Jersey, the Isle of Man and Ireland, and in 2008 a new tax rate for businesses was introduced. This was known as Zero-10, under which the majority of companies in Guernsey would pay no tax on their profits apart from deposit-taking businesses which would pay 10%. However, in 2012, certain elements of the new tax regime were deemed harmful by the European Union's Code of Conduct Group on business taxation (together with those of Jersey and the Isle of Man) and it was repealed. Although the EU had no right to demand the change, the absence of its approval of Guernsey's tax system would have been disastrous. The introduction of Zero-10, and its subsequent withdrawal, resulted in a considerable shortfall in tax revenue and brought about much-needed strict control of States' expenditure which is still in progress.

Conclusion

Guernsey has faced many crises in the past and has often had to adapt to changing circumstances, witness for example the separation from Normandy, the Civil War and the German Occupation. No doubt the island will face more crises in the future but the islanders seem to have an inbuilt resilience to overcome any problems that may arise. The independence retained over the past thousand years is not a prize easily surrendered.

This then completes this short history of our island. Within such a short space inevitably a lot has to be left out, or given at best a brief mention. Criticism there will and should be of a work of this nature, but the author has done his best to outline as accurately and concisely as possible the history of Guernsey in the hope that it will be of interest and use to islanders and visitors alike. One must not forget though that the history of any place, be it island, country or continent cannot be studied in isolation. There are many external factors, happenings and incidents, often many hundreds or thousands of miles away, which can have a drastic influence, either directly or indirectly, on the history of an area. This is particularly so in the case of Guernsey, and it would take many more pages than these to do justice to these external factors and influences.

Market Square, St Peter Port

FURTHER READING

This short history is only able to offer a brief introduction to many of the aspects of Guernsey's past. If you would like to explore any of the topics covered in further detail, this section contains details of some of the best books, the majority of which are still in print, or can be found in local libraries.

General

Transactions of La Société Guernesiaise, (1882 to present)

Review of The Guernsey Society, (1945 to present)

Hocart, Richard *Guernsey's Countryside*, La Société Guernesiaise (2010)

De Garis, Marie *Folklore of Guernsey*, La Société Guernesiaise (1975)

Marr, James *A History of the Bailiwick of Guernsey: The Islanders' Story*, Guernsey Press, (2nd Edition 2001)

Marr, James *Guernsey People*, Phillimore (1984)

Jamieson, A G (ed) *A People of the Sea, The Maritime History of the Channel Islands*, Methuen (1986)

Guernsey on the Map, Priaulx Library (2004)

The Guernsey Farmhouse, a survey by members of the Guernsey Society, De La Rue (1964)

McCormack, John *The Guernsey House*, Phillimore (1980)

Tupper, Ferdinand Brock, *History of Guernsey and its Bailiwick: with occasional notices of Jersey*, Barbet (1854)

Introduction

Ogier, Darryl *The Government and Law of Guernsey*, States of Guernsey (2nd Edition 2012)

States of Guernsey web site, www.gov.gg

Early History

Sebire, Heather *The Archaeology and Early History of the Channel Islands* The History Press (2005)

Feudalism and the Middle Ages

Le Patourel, J H *The Mediaeval Administration of the Channel Islands 1199-1399*, Oxford University Press (1937)

Stevens Cox, Gregory *The Church in Guernsey 1000 AD - 1500AD*, Toucan press (2012)

Separation from Normandy

Eaglestone, AJ *The Channel Islands Under Tudor Government 1485-1642*, Guernsey Society (1949)

Thornton, Tim *The Charters of Guernsey*, Woodfield Publishing (2004)

Ogier, Darryl *Reformation and Society in Guernsey*, Boydell Press (1997)

Pitts, J Linwood *Witchcraft and Devil Lore in the Channel Islands*, Guille-Alles Library (1886)

Thornton, Tim *The Channel Islands 1370 - 1640*, Boydell Press (2012)

Civil War Period

Le Patourel, JH *The Building of Castle Cornet, Guernsey*, Royal Court (1958)

Parker, Bruce *A History of Elizabeth College*, Elizabeth College (2011)

Trade: Privateering and Smuggling

Stevens-Cox, Gregory *St Peter Port 1680-1830: the History of an International Entrepôt*, Boydell Press (1999)

Stevens-Cox, *Guernsey Merchants and their World*, Toucan Press (2010)

Island Defences: The Napoleonic Era

Parks, Major E *Royal Guernsey Militia: A Short History and List of Officers*, La Société Guernesiaise (1992)

Shayer, David *James Saumarez*, La Société Guernesiaise (2006)

Nineteenth Century Guernsey

Hocart, Richard *Peter De Havilland: Bailiff of Guernsey*, La Société Guernesiaise (1997)

Crossan, Rose-Marie *Guernsey 1814-1914: Migration and Modernisation*, Boydell Press (2008)

Stevens-Cox, Gregory *Victor Hugo in the Channel Islands*, Toucan Press (1996)

Williams, Caroline *From Sail to Steam: Studies in Nineteenth Century History of the Channel Islands*, Phillimore (2000)

The Twentieth Century and Beyond

Parks, Major E, *Diex Aie: God Help Us – The Guernseymen who Marched Away 1914-18*, States of Guernsey (1992)

Cruickshank, Charles *German Occupation of the Channel Islands*, The History Press (2004)

Sanders, Paul *The British Channel Islands Under German Occuaption 1940-45*, Jersey Heritage Trust (2005)

Mawson, Gillian *Guernsey Evacuees*, The History Press (2012)

A CHRONOLOGY OF GUERNSEY HISTORY

BC

c 8000	Changes in sea levels separate Guernsey from the European mainland.
c 6500	Evidence of hunting and fishing in Guernsey.
c 4000	Evidence of settlements and farming.
c 2000	Earliest defence earthworks at Jerbourg.

AD

c 150	Evidence of Roman settlement in Guernsey.
c 600	Arrival of St Samson in Guernsey.
867	The Channel Islands became part of Breton kingdom.
933	Channel Islands came under the control of the Dukes of Normandy.
1028	Division of Guernsey into the two large Fiefs held by two Norman Overlords.
1066	William, Duke of Normandy and the Channel Islands conquered England.
1175	John Count of Mortain appointed *Seigneur des Isles* (Lord of the Isles).
1200	Lordship of the Islands given to Pierre des Préaux by King John.
1204	King John driven out of Normandy by the French. Building of Castle Cornet.
1213	King John granted constitutions to the Islands.
1214	Eustace the Monk's unsuccessful attempt to capture Guernsey.
1248	Enquiry into the customs and feudal servitudes by Henry III.
1259	Henry III surrendered title of Duke of Normandy over the ex-Norman possessions. He retained the title with regard to the Channel Islands.
1279	Seal engraved with the Royal Arms granted by Edward I issued for use on all official documents.
1338	Admiral Bahuchet captured Guernsey for the French.
1340	French driven out of Guernsey. They held on to Castle Cornet.
1346	Capture of six English ships and death of crews at the hands of Maron Le Maronier resulted in recapture of Castle Cornet by Geoffrey de Harcourt.
1350	Edward III ordered St Peter Port to be enclosed by a wall.
1356	Island and Castle Cornet captured by the French. Driven out by a force of Jerseymen under the command of the Warden of the Isles.

1372	*La Descente des Arougousais*: Evan of Wales attacks Guernsey. Bloody battle fought above St Peter Port. Castle Cornet and Vale Castle besieged.
1416	Confiscation of Alien Priories by the Crown. (Henry V).
1471	Post of Lord or Keeper and Warden of the Isles abolished. Separate Governors appointed for Guernsey and Jersey.
1480	Papal Bull of Neutrality granted by Pope Sixtus IV.
1556	Burning of Catherine Cauchés and her two daughters at Tower Hill.
1559	Queen Elizabeth I signed the Great Charter which confirmed all the island's rights and privileges granted by King John and confirmed by succeeding Monarchs.
1563	Foundation of Elizabeth College as a grammar school by Queen Elizabeth I.
1565	Colonisation of Sark from Jersey by Helier de Carteret of St Ouen.
1568	Channel Islands transferred from the See of Coutances to that of Winchester, finally severing the French connection.
1570-1610	Governorship of Sir Thomas Leighton.
1572	Arrival of French Huguenots seeking refuge from persecution.
1621	Sir Peter Osborne appointed Governor.
1627	Billeting of 1,200 English soldiers in Guernsey by Charles I.
1643	Parliament issued orders for the arrest of the Governor, Sir Peter Osborne. Orders not carried out and Royal Court dissolved by Parliament. Siege of Castle Cornet held by the Royalist Governor began. Guernsey supported Parliament. Three Jurats imprisoned in the Castle on 28th October. They managed to escape on 3rd December, hours before their intended execution.
1651	Castle Cornet, last Royalist stronghold in the British Isles, surrendered on December 19th.
1660	Restoration of the Monarchy. Charles II restored Guernsey's rights and privileges, the fate of which had been in the balance.
1661-71	Exile of Parliamentarian General Lambert in Castle Cornet.
1672	Explosion at Castle Cornet destroyed central tower and other buildings nearby, including the Governor's residence.
1685	Revocation of the Edict of Nantes resulting in arrival of more Huguenots.
1689	William of Orange proclaimed King of England. Catholic officers and soldiers in the island disarmed.
1694	Award of medal to Privateer Captain John Tupper.
1707	Attempt by British Government to set up a Custom House resisted.
1724	Coal fire established on Casquet rocks as warning light.
1741	Acquisition of land for building of the Town Hospital.

1744	English flagship Victory under command of Admiral Balcher wrecked on the Casquets with loss of 1,100 soldiers and marines.
1757	Birth of James de Saumarez. Entered British Navy and rose to become Commander-in-Chief, Plymouth.
1766	Birth of John Gaspard Le Marchant. Entered British Army and rose to rank of Major-General. Founder of Sandhurst Military College. Killed at Salamanca, 1812.
1769	Birth of Isaac Brock. Entered British Army and rose to rank of Major-General. Killed fighting the French at Battle of Queenston Heights, Canada, 1812.
1777	Building of the Assembly Rooms in St Peter Port, later became Guille-Allès Library.
1780	Red uniform worn for the first time by the Militia.
1782-1812	Building of Fort George.
1783	Mutiny of Irish Regiment at Fort George. Quelled by the Town Regiment of the Guernsey Militia.
1786	Visit of the Duke of Richmond, Master-General of the Ordnance.
1787	Visit of John Wesley. Establishment of Methodism in the island. William Gardner's map of Guernsey, the first accurate survey of Guernsey as a result of the Duke of Richmond's visit.
1788	Birth of archaeologist, Frederick Corbin Lukis.
1789	Opening of the Holy Trinity Church in Trinity Square, second church in town at this date. French Revolution, 14th July.
1791	*La Gazette de Guernesey*, the island's first regular newspaper is published.
1793	Birth of Thomas de la Rue, printer, at Le Bourg.
1794	Planned French invasion of the Channel Islands called off. Establishment of the Post Office in Guernsey. Naval action fought off West Coast by Captain James de Saumarez.
1799	Russian troops billeted in Delancey Barracks.
1800	First Island census - 16,155 people.
1803	Guernsey Lifeboat Station established
1803-16	Governorship of Major-General Doyle.
1807	Draining of Braye du Valle. Beginning of network of main roads by Doyle.
1811	Completion of the Town Prison. Previously prisoners kept in Castle Cornet.
1812	Deaths of Brock and Le Marchant, killed in action.
1817	Formation of the Society of Agriculture, forerunner of the Royal Guernsey Agricultural & Horticultural Society

1820	Building of the States Market and issue of first Guernsey £1 notes.
1821-42	Bailiffship of Daniel de Lisle Brock, brother of Isaac.
1822	States Market opened.
1823	Arrival of first steam ship in Guernsey, the Medina. Commencement of first regular service.
1829	End of Livres Tournois, sols and derniers as island currency. Replaced by francs and centimes.
1830	Guernsey mints its first coins - 1 double and 4 doubles. Gas lighting used for the first time in St Peter Port.
1831	Title of Royal granted to Guernsey Militia by William IV.
1832	Cholera outbreak in St Peter Port. 99 deaths. Cochrane's map of Guernsey printed.
1835	Le Boutillier's Arcade under construction in St Peter Port. Post of Governor abolished. Lieutenant Governors appointed.
1842	Appointment of Sir William Napier as Lieutenant Governor.
1846	First Royal Visit - Queen Victoria and Prince Albert. Erection of Victoria Tower to commemorate the visit.
1853	Laying of foundation stone of new St Peter Port Harbour.
1855	Arrival of Victor Hugo to begin 15 years of exile. Bréhon Tower constructed on rock in the Little Russel.
1859	Second visit of Queen Victoria. Foundation of Les Hanois Lighthouse.
1862-63	Bathing places at Les Terres constructed.
1863	Statue erected to Prince Albert on the pier named after him.
1866	Death of Thomas de la Rue in London. Publication of *Les Travailleurs de la Mer* (Toilers of the Sea) by Victor Hugo, dedicated to the people of Guernsey.
1873	Opening of St Julian's Avenue.
1877	Establishment of present Casquet Lighthouse.
1879	Steam tramway opened, running between Town and St Sampson's.
1881	Lifeboat house built on Castle Emplacement. Guernsey Herd Book Council established to protect Guernsey breed of cattle.
1883	Impressionist painter Pierre-Auguste Renoir spends a month in Guernsey painting 15 pictures of views of Moulin Huet bay and beach.
1889	Arrival of first modern mail boats.

1897	Guernsey Telephone Council granted a licence to operate a telephone system in the island independent of the UK.
1900	First modern motor buses made their appearance.
1905	Inaugural Muratti Vase, annual football tournament between Jersey, Guernsey and Alderney.
1911	States Office built on North Plantation.
1916	Royal Guernsey Militia disbanded. Royal Guernsey Light Infantry formed.
1917	Battle of Cambrai - first major battle of RGLI
1918	RGLI suffer heavy casualties at Battle of Lys
1918	Sea plane used to fly English newspapers in on day of issue.
1922	Introduction of income tax at 6d. in the pound. First Guernsey Eisteddfod Festival
1925	Introduction of first Social Insurance Law.
1927	Formation of Guernsey Amateur Dramatic & Operatic Society by Lady Sackville-West, wife of the Lieutenant-Governor
1928	Completion of New Jetty at the White Rock. Calcutta flying boat established first passenger service from the Castle Emplacement.
1934	Closure of the tramway owing to competition from motor buses.
1935	Completion of the Val des Terres road.
1939	Opening of La Villiaze Airport. Work commenced on reservoir at St Saviour's.
1940	Island demilitarised - Evacuation of 17,000 people. Germans occupied the island in July. Widespread construction begins of bunkers and other defences around the island as part of Hitler's Atlantic Wall
1942	Deportation of 1,000 islanders to prison camps in Germany in retaliation for the British imprisonment of German nationals working in Iran
1943	Formation of the Guernsey Society in London by Sir Donald Banks
1944	Island near to starvation; saved by arrival of Red Cross supply ship Vega from Portugal on December 27th.
1945	Vice-Admiral Huffmeier, German Commander-in-Chief, surrendered on May 9th. Arrival of British troops. Evacuees start returning.
1947	Completion of St Saviour's reservoir.
1948	Constitution Reform Bill altering composition of the States.
1949	Princess Elizabeth Hospital opened at Le Vauquiédor.
1958	Fort George bought by the States, sold to UK development company for luxury housing three years later.

1959	Income tax reduced from 25% to 20%. Tektronix establish manufacturing facility at La Villiaze
1961	Arrival of new mail boats, Sarnia and Caesarea.
1964	Condor Hydrofoil commences inter-island and St. Malo services.
1965	Introduction of States Social Insurance scheme. Abolition of death penalty for all crimes other than treason.
1966	Island Development Committee established.
1968	Aurigny Airlines commence inter-island services.
1969	Take over of British Post Office by the States and issue of first Guernsey stamps by the States. Introduction of restrictions on fishing for ormers – prohibiting diving and limiting ormering to particular tides.
1972	UK signs Treaty of Accession with European Community (EU)
1974	Roll-on/Roll-off terminal established in St Peter Port Harbour.
1976	Beau Sejour Leisure Centre opened.
1978	Discovery of Les Fouaillages prehistoric tomb at L' Ancresse. Completion of Guernsey's first purpose-built museum and art gallery at Candie Gardens.
1980	British Airways cease operations in Guernsey. PAYE type of Income Tax system is introduced.
1981	Publication of *The Book of Ebenezer Le Page* by GB Edwards
1982	BBC Radio Guernsey goes on the air.
1984	Gallo-Roman wreck discovered off St. Peter Port. Foundation of Specsavers Opticians.
1985	New Guernsey flag design approved by the States.
1986	Sealink Ferries cease all services to the Bailiwick.
1987	Completion of North Beach harbour scheme.
1989	New prison opened at Les Nicolles.
1990	Tektronix close Guernsey operations at La Villiaze
1992	Island FM, the island's first commercial radio station, starts broadcasting.
1993	Town Hospital re-opens as new Police Headquarters. Opening of new States Office, Sir Charles Frossard House.
1994	First island-wide election of Conseillers.
1995	Liberation Monument unveiled by HRH Prince of Wales.
1997	Guernsey digital map (Digimap) established.

1998	Law passed abolishing the office of Conseiller.
1999	Channel Express newspaper plane crash lands on Forest Road – 2 killed. Demolition of the Royal Hotel. Guernsey Press acquired by Jersey-based Guiton Group.
2000	First election of 45 Deputies. Undersea cable laid which links Guernsey to the European Electricity Grid via Jersey.
2001	Guernsey Telecom privatised, sold to Cable & Wireless. Millenium Tapestries go on display at St James Arts Centre.
2002	Opening of first phase of Admiral Park development. Guernsey Brewery ceases brewing in Guernsey. Matt Le Tissier makes his 443rd and final appearance for Southampton FC.
2003	States of Guernsey purchase Aurigny Airlines. Guernsey hosts the 10th Islands Games.
2004	States of Guernsey Machinery of Government reforms introduced. New Airport Terminal opened.
2005	Replica ship mast erected at the bottom of St Julian's Avenue as part of national celebrations of the bicentenary of the Battle of Trafalgar. Andy Priaulx wins first of three World Touring Car championships.
2006	States of Guernsey take over responsibility for Guernsey's bus services. Opening of the new Royal Court building on the site of the former police station & prison. Smoking banned in public places.
2007	British Government responsibility for Channel Islands transferred to Ministry of Justice. Opening of new shopping centre in the redevelopment of the old markets.
2008	Introduction of Zero-10 business tax rates. First Blue Plaque unveiled on the former home of GB Edwards, author of *The Book of Ebenezer Le Page*.
2009	First democratic elections in Sark. Heather Watson wins Girls' Singles title at US Open Tennis.
2010	Waitrose acquires the two largest island supermarkets at Rohais and Admiral Park.
2011	Joint Guernsey & Jersey office established in Brussels to manage relationship with the European Union. Guernsey FC established to compete in the UK league system. They win Combined Counties League and Premier Cup in their first season. Standard of RAF 201 (Guernsey's Own) Squadron laid up at Castle Cornet on the disbandment of the squadron.

2012   Withdrawal of Zero-10 business tax rates following pressure from the European Union
UK Government closes tax relief "loopholes" resulting in the withdrawal of Low Value Consignment Relief (LVCR) concessions and closure of Qualifying Recognised Overseas Pensions (QROPS) business
Carl Hester of Sark wins gold medal as part of Dressage team at London Olympics.

2013   Discovery and disposal of a World War Two mine in Bluebell Wood.
Shipping company Huelin-Renouf ceased trading, as indirect consequence of the removal of LVCR concession.
Flybe withdrew Gatwick - Guernsey air route.
States vote to close St Sampson's Infants and St Andrew's Primary schools.

About the Guernsey Society

Aims and Objectives

The aims of the Guernsey Society are to promote, maintain and stimulate interest in all matters concerning the Bailiwick of Guernsey, the past, present and future, and, thereby, to keep alive the Spirit of Guernsey both in the island and overseas.

The Society was formed in London in 1943 to represent the interests of the occupied islanders and evacuees in the UK to the British Government. Today, the Society has a more social focus, and a worldwide membership. Our activities include:

* publishing a magazine, The Review, three times a year, which contains a wide range of articles about Guernsey's past, present and future.
* organising regular meetings in London and Guernsey.

Membership

Membership is open anyone with a connection to or interest in the Bailiwick of Guernsey.

Find Us Online

For more details visit our web site at **www.guernsey-society.org.uk**, like us on Facebook (facebook.com/guernseysociety) or follow us on Twitter (@guernseysociety).

Visit our Online Bookshop

On our website, you will also find a bookshop which contains a wide selection of books relating to the Bailiwick. **www.guernsey-society.org.uk/bookshop/**

Popular topics include:

- World War II-related books
- Channel Islands Fiction
- Guernsey History
- Natural History & Environment
- Films/DVDs

Donkipedia – the Guernsey encyclopedia

If you are interested in learning more about the Bailiwick of Guernsey, you will find a wide range of interesting articles at our online encyclopedia.

Popular topics include: Guernsey Surnames and Family History, Biographies of prominent Guernseymen and women, others.

It takes its name from Guernsey Donkeys - the traditional nickname for Guernsey people. In the spirit of any wiki – it is open for everyone to share their knowledge of Guernsey People, Places and Heritage.

Sausmarez Manor, an elegant country house built in the Queen Anne style in about 1715-1719